What Matters
MOST
for School Leaders

To Betty J. Patzkowsky, my sister, guardian,
and friend, who taught me a lot about what matters most.

Robert D. Ramsey

What Matters
MOST
for School Leaders

25
Reminders
of What Is Really
IMPORTANT

CORWIN PRESS
A Sage Publications Company
Thousand Oaks, California

For information:

Corwin Press
A Sage Publications Company
2455 Teller Road
Thousand Oaks, California 91320
www.corwinpress.com

SAGE Publications Ltd
1 Oliver's Yard
55 City Road
London EC1Y 1SP
United Kingdom

Sage Publications India Pvt. Ltd.
B-42, Panchsheel Enclave
Post Box 4109
New Delhi 110 017 India

Printed in the United States of America

Library of Congress Cataloging-in-Publication Data

Ramsey, Robert D.
What matters most for school leaders : 25 reminders of what is really important / Robert D. Ramsey.
      p. cm.
Includes index.
ISBN 1-4129-0451-X (hardcover) — ISBN 1-4129-0452-8 (pbk.)
    1. School management and organization—United States—Handbooks, manuals, etc.
2. School administrators—United States. I. Title.
LB2805.R26 2005
371.2′011—dc22

                                                       2004011552

This book is printed on acid-free paper.

05   06   07   08   09   10   9   8   7   6   5   4   3   2   1

Acquisitions Editor:	Elizabeth Brenkus
Editorial Assistant:	Candice L. Ling
Production Editor:	Kristen Gibson
Copy Editor:	Edward Meidenbauer
Typesetter:	C&M Digitals (P) Ltd.
Indexer:	David Luljak
Proofreader:	Sue Irwin
Cover Designer:	Anthony Paular

Contents

Preface

Why This Book? Why Now?

Anything less than a conscientious commitment to the important is an unconscious commitment to the unimportant.

. . . we get busier and busier doing "good" things and never even stop to ask ourselves if what we're doing really matters most.

Stephen R. Covey, award-winning author

It's easy for school administrators to lose their way in today's tumultuous educational environment. There are so many diversions and distractions. So many problems, pressures, and conflicting interests. So many momentary crises. So many regulations. So much paperwork. So much red tape. (Have I left anything out?) It's no wonder that school leaders find it increasingly difficult to stay on track and to keep in mind what really matters most.

How many administrators have you known who entered the profession, the principalship or the superintendency following a star—only to end up mucking around in the mud, lost in the mire of administrivia. None of us want that to happen to our careers.

All principals and superintendents want to keep the main thing the main thing. But like all leaders, school officials need an occasional pep talk or refresher course to rekindle their passion, renew their perspective, refocus on their priorities and revive their sense of purpose. That's why this book was written.

We hear a lot these days about principle-centered leadership and value-driven organizations. But what principles? What values? What are the ideas and ideals that never change?

They are all right here in this single, compact volume. Each page is a wake-up call or heads-up reminding school leaders of the simple, guiding truths and timeless values that made them want to become educators in the first place.

The only way to stay grounded is to remember—to recall what you're about, why you're about it, how it came about, and what it is all about—and, by remembering, keep your priorities straight, keep your head in the game, and do what matters most every day.

Ships need anchors most when seas are roughest. So do school leaders. This book is about anchors.

It is also about reawakening, renewing, refocusing, reconnecting, and recommitting. More important, it is a survival guide for the soul of every school leader. What principal or superintendent doesn't need a boost like that?

There are many books advising administrators about what to do and how to do it. But not many resources remind them of why they are doing it. Most books for school leaders are like tool kits. This one is more like a compass.

You may have heard the old joke about the airline pilot who came over the intercom and informed passengers, "We are lost; but we're making good time." Some schools are like that too. That's where this guide comes in. It is one of the few flight manuals available to help the pilots of the nation's schools avoid deviating from their original flight plan and becoming lost in the process. ("Where you're headed is more important than how fast you're going." —Stephen R. Covey.)

There is always a need for books of practical tips, techniques, and strategies. But there is also an important place for hard-earned wisdom and lasting truths. That's what this book has to offer that is different.

What Matters Most for School Leaders is a compact guide of 25 fundamental insights and baseline beliefs that never change. Basically, it is a primer on what is truly important for today's school leaders at all levels.

Each section showcases a different commonsense cornerstone principle or life lesson of school leadership, reinforced by real-world examples from successful schools and practical tips on how to concentrate on what counts and apply what's most important on the job every day.

This is a how-to book—not how to do the daily chores of school management, but how to stay focused on what really matters.

There is nothing much new in this little book. But there are a lot of forgotten truths—freshly viewed and packaged in modern-day terms—to help school leaders stay the course and stay on course.

What Matters Most for School Leaders is aimed at all school administrators who have ever felt lost and confused, feared they were wasting their time and their careers, or simply asked themselves, "What am I doing here and why am I doing it?" That's just about every principal and superintendent everywhere. If you are one of them, this book is for you. After all, you matter too!

Acknowledgments

Many people helped write this book and don't even know it. They are the principals, superintendents, mentors, colleagues, and friends whose words, actions, examples, and modeling have helped me to appreciate what is really most important for school leaders.

These include: Oscar Haugh, Owen Henson, Carl Knox, Harold Enestvedt, Mike Hickey, Carl Holmstrom, and Carol Johnson.

Of course, there are also a few people who definitely do know they helped with this book. These are my patient and supportive editor, Robb Clouse, who got the project started; and my wife, Joyce Ramsey, whose technical and editorial skills finished it up.

To these (and any others whose contributions I may have inadvertently omitted or overlooked) I am deeply indebted. Thank you! Thank you! Thank you!

In addition, Corwin Press gratefully acknowledges the contributions of the following individuals:

Randel Beaver
Superintendent
Archer City Independent School District
Archer City, TX

Charles Galloway
Professor
Department of Counseling and Educational Leadership
University of North Florida
Jacksonville, FL

Sandy Harris
Assistant Professor
College of Education
Stephen F. Austin State University
Nacogdoches, TX

Gary McCartney
Superintendent of Schools
South Brunswick School District
South Brunswick, NJ

Gina Segobiano
Superintendent/Principal
Signal Hill School District #181
Belleville, IL

Phil Silsby
Principal
Belleville West High School
Belleville, IL

Dana Trevethan
Principal
Turlock High School
Turlock, CA

About the Author

 **Robert D. Ramsey** is a lifelong educator who has served as a "leader of leaders" in three award-winning school districts in two states, including St. Louis Park, Minnesota, where all elementary and secondary schools have been designated by the federal government as National Schools of Excellence.

Ramsey's front-line experience includes positions as teacher, counselor, supervisor, assistant principal, curriculum coordinator, personnel director, assistant superintendent, acting superintendent, and adjunct professor.

Throughout his distinguished career, Ramsey's writings have helped countless educators to achieve greater success. His popular works, *Lead, Follow or Get Out of the Way* and *School Leadership From A-Z*, have been heralded as "must reading" for today's principals and superintendents.

In his latest book, *What Matters Most for School Leaders,* Ramsey again provides insight and inspiration to help busy administrators make the most of their career of choice for a lifetime.

Ramsey and his wife, Joyce, now live in Minneapolis, where he works as a freelance writer and where they can be close to their two children and four grandchildren.

OTHER BOOKS BY ROBERT D. RAMSEY

School Leadership From A-Z (Corwin Press)

Lead, Follow, or Get Out of the Way (Corwin Press)

How to Say the Right Thing Every Time (Corwin Press)

501 Tips for Teachers (Contemporary Books)

Introduction

Some Things Never Change

Just because everything is different doesn't mean anything has changed.

Irene Peters, writer

Don't let complexities obscure responsibilities. . . . Life is simpler when we know what's essential.

Joseph L. Badaracco, *Leading Quietly*

Change is our life. It's what school leaders do. We manage change. We make it happen. If things aren't changing fast enough, we change them.

It's no wonder then that many school administrators feel confused, fragmented, overwhelmed, and stressed out. It is difficult to remain stable and steadfast when everything around you is in a constant state of flux and chaos.

Unfortunately, all principals and superintendents today function in an environment of continuous evolution, revolution, and convolution. In education, everything is constantly changing. Or is it?

Despite appearances, some things never change. And if you want to run a successful school or school system, you need to know what they are—the sooner, the better.

Regardless of proliferating new expectations, new requirements, new regulations, new laws, new court decisions, new trends, new theories, new research, new technology, or new priorities, some basic principles and premises, mercifully, remain the same. If there are any administrators who forget or don't understand this, the next change they hear about may be in their title.

As an educational leader, you may be proud of your ability to be flexible, adaptable, and go with the flow. But also be thankful for the conditions and values that never change. You need them to survive and succeed.

That's why this book is designed as a not-so-gentle reminder that there are still constants in our profession. God bless 'em. We all need them to keep us grounded. Seattle minister and columnist, Dr. Dale Turner, calls them "an inner gyroscope that makes steadiness possible in an environment of rapid transition."

Unfortunately, in the blur of swirling transformations, it is easy to forget or overlook these basic principles and guiding life lessons. That's how some administrators lose their way and allow their careers to drift off course. But it doesn't have to happen.

Even professional athletes occasionally need to be reminded to keep their eye on the goal and to avoid getting distracted by the bright lights, the noise, the scoreboard, the media, or the fans. That's where coaches come in.

As it turns out, all professionals—including school leaders—need similar reminders. That's where this little book comes in.

The following pages contain fixed truths you can count on today—and tomorrow—and every other day from now on, no matter what else changes. Revisit them. If they sound familiar, they are. After all, they are what matters most for school leaders.

1 What You Do Is Special

If you're lost, the Principal shows you the way.

Unidentified primary student

Some readers won't believe a word of this chapter. A few of these naysayers may even be principals or superintendents. But if you are one of them, run—don't walk—to the nearest career counselor. You're in the wrong job!

Never belittle your position as a school leader. There is no such thing as "just" a principal or superintendent. What you do is special!

We hear a lot about leaders in other fields (e. g., CEOs, generals, and elected officials) being important and influential role models. But school administrators aren't exactly "chopped liver" themselves.

In fact, not many—if any—positions of leadership are as important to the future of the community and the nation as the school principalship or superintendency. (And by the way, the elementary principalship just may be the best leadership job in the country.)

Never underestimate the significance of your role. If you do, so will everyone else. When you devalue your position you demean the entire profession.

When I think of school leaders, I'm often reminded of an off-hand comment my college roommate made years ago. While telling me about working on a summer construction job with a group of administrators who were moonlighting from their school-year assignments, my roommate remarked, "I had forgotten how special school principals are."

That observation stuck with me. It still rings true. Throughout a lifelong career in education, it has been reinforced countless times.

I also recall another conversation years later when a brash, ambitious, and talented young teacher at Topeka (Kansas) West High School confronted his principal, Dr. Owen Henson, saying, "I can go to work with a major insurance company and, in 3 years, I'll make more money than you do."

Henson simply replied, "That's probably true, but we will both still know who has the most important job."

Henson was right. And incidentally, the young teacher later became a successful principal in his own right.

Naturally, it's no great revelation that school administrators don't make as much money as leaders in many other fields. But in our heart of hearts, most of us know that income isn't the primary measure of importance. Jesus, Gandhi, Schweitzer, and Mother Teresa weren't big moneymakers either. Yet no one questions their impact or the lasting significance of their contributions.

Maybe the following vignette makes the point best:

First CEO: "I make a six-figure salary."

Second CEO: "I make a six-figure salary plus stock options and bonuses."

School Principal: "I make a difference."

If you need something even more objective to establish the special status of school leaders, try looking up the definition of your job title. My dog-eared copy of the *American Heritage Dictionary of the English Language* (Houghton Mifflin, Third Edition) lists these definitions:

Principal: 1. First, highest or foremost in importance, rank, worth, or degree; chief—One who holds a position of presiding rank.

Superintendent: 1. A person with the authority to supervise and direct.

Wow! Would the dictionary lie?

What principals and superintendents do is undeniably distinctive and exceptional because—

- School leaders perform both leadership and management functions.
- School leaders are accountable to many "bosses."
- School leaders function in a "fishbowl" and make daily decisions in full view of all of the stakeholders involved.
- School leaders exercise a wide span of control, play to diverse audiences, and serve a broad range of intergenerational constituencies.
- School leaders make choices and decisions that affect many segments of the community.
- School leaders deal daily with the community's most precious resource.
- School leaders directly help shape the future and leave a lasting legacy.

No other category of leadership can make these statements. What all school leaders do is special. Point made. Case closed.

That's why it is important that administrators resist taking their role for granted. School leadership isn't just another job. It matters more than most other executive positions.

Serving as a principal or superintendent is a unique opportunity to influence the lives of individual children and the fortunes of the entire community at the same time. Overstated? I don't think so. And neither should you. Being a school leader may not be a sacred calling. But it comes close.

The best way to begin each day is simply to remember the reasons for what you do. They are what set you apart from ordinary managers and supervisors. Good leaders are always purpose-driven. Don't forget yours. Never allow yourself to miss the point of being an educator.

If you lose sight of the extraordinary nature of what you do and why you do it, or trivialize the significance of your work, or allow yourself to be intimidated or feel inferior in the company of other leaders, you risk losing your edge and diminishing your passion for the job.

That's unacceptable. Your students, your employers, and your community deserve better. If you can't respect what you do, it's time to do something else.

Whenever your faith or passion begin to waiver, just look in the face of a kindergartener on the first day of school, observe the love at work in a special education class, or attend a commencement ceremony (especially a GED graduation) and see the pride in the eyes of every student—and every parent.

These are everyday experiences for educators. But they are also surefire faith restorers. They work every time. And they cannot be duplicated in any other position or profession.

After all, you have the job most CEOs would be afraid to touch. Not just anyone can do it. Not even every successful teacher can become an effective principal or superintendent. So instead of soft-pedaling your role, you should do everything possible to articulate and exemplify the importance of effective school leaders.

As a case in point, years ago when I first earned a doctorate in education, I insisted on using the title, "Doctor," not because of any self-serving delusions of grandeur, but because the public needed to appreciate that public schools require and are entitled to leaders as well-educated and well-qualified as those in any other essential public institution. The job is too important to be left to just any retrofitted teacher who has become tired of the classroom.

By now, that point has pretty much been made. Titles are no longer an issue. Today, there are more and better ways to honor and validate the importance of school leaders. The following seventeen suggestions illustrate how you can become a better leader of your particular school while enhancing the image of all professional educational leaders at the same time:

1. Refuse to engage in self-promotion, petty politics, or any other questionable practices. Model integrity, honesty, and dignity on and off the job. School leaders are often held to a higher standard (perhaps because theirs is a higher calling). Don't fret it or sweat it. Just clear the bar every time. People will notice.

2. Stop whining. Educators are notorious complainers. It doesn't help (although there's a lot to gripe about). Bellyaching is never an effective leadership technique in any field. You want respect, not pity. The way to get it is to deal with adversity, solve tough problems, prove you can do more with less and still deliver on your commitments.

3. Delegate routine and mundane activities to subordinates. Assign record keeping and paper shuffling to others. Spend your time on issues, ideas, and ideals that truly make a difference. If you spend your days on menial tasks, people will think you have a menial job. It's a mistake many administrators make. It's always easy (and comfortable) to fill your time with details, trifles, and minutia. But busyness isn't leadership.

4. Let people in on what you do and deal with every day. Make public the issues and problems facing you. And the solutions. Hold neighborhood "town meetings" and on-site coffee klatches for parents. Start a Dad's Club in your school to get more fathers involved. If possible, initiate a weekly call-in radio show or a community access TV program. When people ask, "What do you do all summer?" have an answer. Community members need to know that school leaders don't just preside over glorified baby-sitting services or manage warehouses for kids. It's your job to teach them. Society can't appreciate, respect, or support what it doesn't know about.

5. Initiate "shadow" or "principal-for-a-day" programs. Let staff and community members see first-hand what it really takes to run a school or a school district. In Minnesota, even Governor Tim Pawlenty has been known to "walk in the shoes" of a school principal for a day. It can't hurt to have government officials gain appreciation for the successes and challenges principals face every day.

6. Tap local CEOs and other business leaders as mentors for principals. The business community can help principals learn new leadership

and decision-making skills while gaining greater insight into the real-world challenges of school leadership. It's not uncommon for mentors to learn more than they teach.

7. Recruit top talent to the profession. Right now, there is a dearth of qualified leadership coming through the pipeline. That's scary. The principalship and superintendency are exceptional jobs—but only if filled by exceptional men and women. Mediocre administrators give the profession a bad name and shortchange the future. We can do better. We have to.

8. Urge the school board to publicly showcase and recognize outstanding administrators on a regular basis.

9. Work to eliminate the employment of part-time principals or the assignment of one administrator to serve more than one school in your district or any other school system.

10. Better yet, lobby for legislation requiring a qualified leader (principal) in every school. Minnesota state law used to mandate a full-time principal in every school of a certain size. Unfortunately, the legislative standard was changed from mandatory to permissive. It's amazing how much difference changing the word *shall* to *may* can make. This wasn't perfect legislation; but it was a pretty good model. Now, it's just wishful thinking.

11. If your state has a statutory ceiling cap on superintendents' salaries, work to eliminate it. My home state has experimented with limiting the pay of all public employees (including school leaders) to no more than 95% of the governor's salary. It doesn't work. The state hasn't attracted any better governors and has lost a number of excellent school administrators in the process. As it turns out, leadership (even school leadership) is a competitive business too. You pretty much get what you pay for.

12. Likewise, never apologize for how much you make. Effective leadership costs money. It's worth it. The sooner society accepts this fact the better.

13. Support professional organizations, such as NAESP, NASSP, and ASCD, that recognize, support and are advocates for school leaders.

14. Challenge the common media depiction of school administrators as stuffy, stupid, ineffectual, or worse. (Remember *Ferris Buehler's Day Off?*)

15. Become visible in community activities. Join a civic or service club. Coach Little League. Get involved in church and charity activities. It helps for everyone in the community—not just parents—to know who their school leaders are.

16. Make yourself known to power brokers (e.g., media representatives, city officials, and legislators). Networking shouldn't be limited exclusively to other educators. Having important contacts is never a liability.

17. Be aggressive in telling your school's story. When influential people think of good schools, you want them to think of you and your school first.

Of course, the best way to underscore the special nature and value of school leadership is to be the best principal or superintendent you can be.

Do real work. Talk about real issues. Face facts. Do what's right, not just what's safe. Be the all-time, number one champion of putting children first.

Be the voice for kids that won't shut up or go away. When you do, people see your job in a whole different light—and that's a good thing. The point is that whatever you do to boost the image and understanding of your special role in your school and community also enhances the perception of all school leaders.

Curriculums come and go. So do teaching materials. But one thing remains fixed—the critical need for effective school leadership.

Schools can only be as strong as the leaders who guide them. Good leaders make good teaching and learning possible. You may have a bad school with a good leader; but you can't have a good school with a bad leader.

If the public schools fail, it won't be because of lack of funding or public support. It will be because of a lack of leadership. How scary is that? And how uniquely important does that make your job?

The next time you question your career choice, remember what makes what you do unique. Here are a few final reminders:

- You get to feed off the energy of youth every day. (Who can get old on a job like that?)
- You hear more laughter in a day than most leaders do in a week. (Kids laugh an average of 150 times a day; adults only 15 times.)
- You witness firsthand the thrill and excitement of learning and participate in miracles on a daily basis.
- You play an important role in shaping tomorrow's leaders (and followers).

- You get to play a vital part in the largest youth-serving organization in the nation and to lead the most important public institution in your community.
- More important, you get to be there when young people find out who they are and who they can be.

It doesn't get any more special than that! And that's one thing that will never change.

2 Primero Los Ninos

Children First

Mankind owes to the children the best it has to offer.

United Nations Charter

If America hopes to secure its future, children must come first.

Ernest Boyer, educator-author

The way to build a stronger America is to build stronger, better families. Our children must come first.

Barbara Bush, Former First Lady

The nurturance of children is at risk.

Marian Wright Edelman,
Founder of the Children's Defense Fund

The children must come first. To some, this may sound like a platitude. But for all educators, it must be a nonnegotiable, irrevocable, ironclad core value. Many precepts are important. This one is essential.

In fact, the primacy of children is so fundamental and so self-evident that I almost didn't even include it in this book at all. It seems almost too obvious to mention. So why is it here? Because there are still people out there who don't believe that kids should be our top priority. Unfortunately, some of them actually work in schools. You probably have a few on your payroll as you read these words.

Many adults merely give lip service to making children a priority. Some don't even do that much. We all know men and women who don't like kids, don't trust kids, don't want to be around kids, and are even downright afraid of kids (especially teenagers). Some adults actually suffer from misopedia—the hatred of children, including their own.

Most of these people believe children should be treated as second-class citizens (e.g., "seen and not heard") and that kids' needs or interests should take a backseat to the desires of adults. If you don't believe that such feelings can and do exist among school personnel, you may want to consider hiring a reality coach.

If you still have doubts, try answering these questions: Have you ever known a school leader who placed politics over students' needs? Or one who settled for what the school board wanted rather than for what would benefit students most? Do you know any principals who act as if the school revolves around them? Or teachers who think they are the most important person in their classroom? Or have you ever observed a school organized and operated for the convenience of adults instead of for what helps kids most? If you're like most of us, the correct answer to all of the above is a resounding "Yes"!

The unvarnished truth is that not all school employees put children first. That's why you, as school leader, have to. If there is a moral imperative in this business, this is it.

Even those of us who are staunch champions of children need occasional reminders. Just because a baseline principle is a given, it doesn't mean that you can't take it for granted. And anything taken for granted can easily be ignored or forgotten. (That's why, sometimes, what goes without saying should be said anyway.)

I know this is true because I am as prone as anyone to overlooking the obvious. In truth, the only reason that the importance of valuing children over all else finally ended up in these pages at all is that I recently attended a graduation ceremony. It was a "Celebracion de Transicion Sexto Grado" for sixth graders at a local Spanish immersion school. The class was the first to complete all grades in the school.

The event was a particularly emotional affair as students, parents, and teachers celebrated achieving a major milestone. It was a joyous tribute to what can be accomplished when all parties work together to put children first. In fact, the stated theme for the event was "Primero los Ninos"—Children First! Participating in that celebration was a wake-up call for me. It forcibly reminded me anew of what my life and my career are all about. Now, I'm reminding you.

No self-respecting principal or superintendent can afford to forget—even for a little while—that all great nations place great emphasis on their children. It's called survival. ("The greatest natural resource that any nation can have is its children." —Danny Kaye, actor-comedian.)

Unfortunately, our society isn't doing too well by its young people at present. You know and have seen the signs. Marian Wright Edelman may say it best, "It is a spiritually impoverished nation that permits infants and children to be the poorest Americans."

That's why it is more important than ever for school leaders to become the conscience of the community regarding children. If it is not in your job description, it should be.

And like any good conscience, you may need to nag, scold, coax, cajole, and kick butt at times if that's what it takes to protect and promote the value of children and youth in our nation. Anything less is selling short at best and selling out at worst.

Like it or not, it is your responsibility to marshal and motivate the entire village to value and help raise all its children. But how?

Fortunately, there are boundless ideas and opportunities to engage people in putting children above other concerns. You already are aware of many of them. And I have one more you should know about.

I currently live in a self-proclaimed "Children First" community. My hometown, St. Louis Park, Minnesota, was the first community in the nation to use the Search Institute's groundbreaking research on developmental assets as the basis for forging a citywide partnership (e.g., city government, schools, businesses, health care providers and the faith community) to promote a better future for all young people and a healthier community for all ages. Nearly 600 other communities nationwide have now undertaken similar approaches.

The Minneapolis-based Search Institute has identified and validated 40 essential developmental assets (see examples) that all children and teens need to survive and thrive at school and in life. (Most kids in America have less than half.)

Search Institute's Developmental Assets

(Example)

External Assets	*Internal Assets*
Family support	Motivation
Positive family communication	Helping others
Caring neighborhood	Integrity
Community values youth	Responsibility
Useful roles	Behavioral restraint
Family boundary	Resistance skills
Adult role models	Peaceful conflict resolution
Positive peers	Self-esteem
High expectations	Sense of purpose
Sports, clubs, etc.	Positive view of
Religious community	personal future

The complete list is available from the Search Institute, 700 S. Third St., Suite 210, Minneapolis, MN 55415

Search's research shows that the more of these assets children have, the more likely they are to succeed. Conversely, the fewer assets in a child's life, the greater likelihood of at-risk and antisocial behavior (e.g., smoking, alcohol and drug use, gang membership, violence, etc.) Increase the number of assets and kids get along better and achieve more. Reduce assets and kids begin to slip, falter, and fail. It works every time.

St. Louis Park now has over 10 years of experience with a homegrown initiative (labeled—can you believe it?—"Children First") designed to engage everyone in the community as active asset-builders for children and youth. The initiative is not a specific program or set of services, but rather an open-ended call to all citizens to support children in every way they can. The emphasis is on building up strengths instead of remedying weaknesses. It seems to be working.

Repeated follow-up studies show a consistent increase in the number of assets among St. Louis Park youth. More kids have more assets and are thriving more than ever before. This is solid evidence that asset-building can have a lasting impact. As Penn State University researcher, Dr. Craig Edel Brock, reports, "Children First in St. Louis Park has now moved from pioneering to history and from unparalleled to precedent-setting."

The message is too important to go unheard. Building assets in kids works. Guaranteed. It can make a difference in any community, including yours.

Of course, you don't have to launch a full-scale, community-wide mobilization effort in order to begin putting children first. There are lots of smaller scale ideas that have succeeded in schools and communities just like yours. These are approaches that can be adopted or adapted in almost any situation:

- Sponsor an annual Youth Summit where grown-ups listen to what kids are really thinking and feeling.
- Include youth representatives on school and city committees, commissions, and task forces (e.g., let children help design school playgrounds or their own skateboard park).
- Help students compile *An Adult's Guide to Kids* containing advice on what support kids need from grown-ups. If this doesn't start an intergenerational dialogue, nothing will.
- Assist with the creation of a school and/or community foundation to supplement and enhance financial support to benefit all students. You might be surprised at how many alumni and staff retirees are receptive to estate-planning that includes an endowment to help kids.

- Educate adults (including school personnel) about how to talk to kids.
  Here are some clues from students themselves:

  > Don't keep asking, "How's school?" or gushing over "How big
  > we're getting!"
  > Don't preach, nag, or trivialize our pop culture.
  > Be honest.
  > Talk about common interests (e.g., movies, books, or current
  > events.)

- Provide training for volunteer community coaches (and fans) on how
  to stress sportsmanship over winning and having fun over cutthroat
  competition.
- Encourage community clergy to develop a common statement of core
  values for children that all faiths and denominations can agree upon.
  It's not easy, but some communities have succeeded in doing it.
- Reach out to immigrants and other newcomers through a New Student
  Help Center which offers assistance with orientation, registration,
  paperwork, and other special help before school ever starts. Such a
  center is a big hit in St. Paul and can work in your community as well.
- Set up an afterschool drop-in center ("Drop Zone") where secondary
  students can workout, swim, shoot hoops, get help with homework, or
  just hang out with friends. Supervised afterschool activities are better
  than cruising the streets, loitering around the mall, or just going home,
  watching TV, and waiting for parents to get off work. The hours immediately after school are often the most deadly and dangerous for kids,
  so what better way to put children first than to keep them safe.
- Promote creation of neighborhood scholarships to support advanced
  education or training for deserving kids.
- Lobby local businesses to avoid treating students as suspects. If kids
  are required to check backpacks or carrying cases before shopping, all
  customers should be subjected to the same requirement. Otherwise, it
  feels like discrimination to young people.
- Seek funding to adopt a "no-cut" policy for school sports programs.
  Too often, the kids who need the benefits of organized sports the most
  are the ones who are deprived of the opportunity to play.
- Involve kids in planning family activities for block parties on National
  Night Out.
- Encourage working families to create periodic "sneak outs" where
  one parent and one child go out for a movie, dinner, or a ball game.
- Urge key business leaders to finance efforts to attract the strongest
  teachers to struggling schools and to keep good educators in urban
  (inner city) schools.

- We've all seen bumper stickers admonishing us to "Start Seeing Motorcycles." Why not initiate a "Start Seeing Kids" campaign by challenging adults to notice kids, talk to kids, and even learn the names of all the kids on their block?
- Pester city officials to enforce student curfew ordinances to keep kids off the streets and keep them safe and out of trouble late at night.
- Encourage employers and parents to limit student work-for-pay jobs to 20 hours per week.
- Provide leadership for developing a network of bike trails crisscrossing the community so that young people can get around safely and conveniently.
- Develop a Respect Code to hold both students and adults accountable for civil and respectful behavior toward others.
- Schedule school events, parties, games, practices, and rehearsals to allow families some regular evening time together.
- Introduce an "All in the Family Day" to celebrate the diversity and variety of types of families living in the community.

The list could go on and on, but you get the idea. Keeping children a top priority requires an accumulation of many actions, great and small. ("Nothing done for a child is ever wasted." –Attributed to public radio icon, Garrison Keillor)

If you need further convincing and are one of those readers who enjoys a good metaphor, the following vignette may make my point about putting children first best of all:

One evening a small boy sat on the floor working on a giant jigsaw puzzle, while his father sat nearby engrossed in a newspaper. The picture in the puzzle was of a little boy standing on top of the globe.

It was a difficult puzzle with hundreds of pieces. Consequently, the boy kept asking his father for help, but the father repeatedly replied, "In a minute."

Sometime later, when the father finished his paper, he went to check on his son's progress with the puzzle. To his surprise, he found the puzzle completed—every piece in place—and his son grinning from ear to ear.

"Wow," said the father. "How did you finish the puzzle all by yourself?"

"Well," replied the son. "I just concentrated on putting the little boy in the picture together right and, then, the whole world came out right!"

Strangely enough, it's no puzzle that it works that way in the real world as well.

Children come first. There is no close second. That's why all children are deserving of sacrifice. ("We must all work to make the world worthy of its children."–Pablo Casals, Spain's world-class cellist.) As a school administrator, you should know this better than anyone and act on it every day, on and off the job.

You'll know you've got it right when you wake up every morning and fall in love with children all over again.

If you want more detailed information on building assets in kids, please contact Karen Atkinson, Children First Coordinator, 6425 W. 33rd St., St. Louis Park, MN 55426.

3 There Are No Throwaway Kids

The essence of our effort to see that every child has a chance must be to insure each an equal opportunity, not to become equal, but to become different.

John Fischer, child advocate

Well, I guess the children have left for school by this time.

F. Scott Fitzgerald, American novelist

Every child can learn. And it's your job to make it happen. If that doesn't scare you away, you have the makings of a good school leader.

There are no throwaway kids in public schools. That's why we call them "public." Every kid counts.

George W. Bush had it right when he campaigned for the presidency on the promise to "leave no child behind." But it wasn't a new idea. That has always been the promise of America's schools and their leaders.

If you are looking for something to get passionate about, stop looking. This is it—every child gets a chance. Not just some children or most children, but all children!

You are not the principal or superintendent for just the good kids, the bright kids, the well-scrubbed kids, the well-behaved kids, or the privileged kids. You are the leader of a school for all children—including the unmotivated kids, the slow kids, the sick and disabled kids, the smelly kids, the troubled kids, the abused kids, the scared kids, the angry kids, the kids in gangs, the kids using drugs, and the kids on welfare. No matter how small your school is it has to be big enough for everyone.

Wow! They should give out gold stars for a job like that. (Maybe they do.)

Sound overwhelming? It is. But true leaders take overwhelming in stride, do it anyway and ask for more. If you think the job is too big, you may not be big enough for the job.

Unconditional, unflinching inclusiveness is what sets your school apart from other learning organizations. You have to accept everyone, keep everyone, and educate everyone. If they don't come to you, you have to go out and round them up. There must be a little bit of shepherd in every public school administrator.

There are no lost lambs, strays, or throwaway kids in this business. As school leader, you must welcome and work with all abilities, emotional states, economic levels, religious faiths, and racial backgrounds. You cannot allow any child to be neglected, forgotten, ignored, overlooked, or abandoned.

Whoa. Now slow down a bit. Dwell on this thought a moment, and let it sink in. This is a huge deal.

There is nothing more important than providing optimal education to the children—all children. And no child is more important than another. None are disposable or dispensable. These should be the bedrock beliefs that get you going every day of your life. This is what makes your job meaningful.

As a school leader, you have a multitude of decisions, great and small, to make every day. But you have only one standard or criteria to apply: What's best for kids?! That's what's most important.

If I had to come up with a tag line for the public's schools, I might borrow from the city of Key West, Florida. Key West is the only municipality in the nation to adopt "One Human Family" as its official motto and mantra—and mean it. This could well be the signature statement and rallying cry for your school as well.

A commitment to providing not just something but the right thing for every child is a core value for all effective school leaders. It can't be amended or modified. It's not a fad. It's a fixture.

As a principal or superintendent, if you want to devote your energies to something that really matters, keep looking for new and better ways to meet the individual needs of *all* pupils. It's that simple.

To help get you in the right mindset, following is a sampling of suggestions many successful schools have used to differentiate, individualize, personalize, customize, and humanize the educational experience for all learners. Some are tried and true. Others are only trials.

The list is intended to be suggestive, not exhaustive. If you are already doing some or all of these things, take a bow. If you see some that you want to borrow or build on, help yourself. They're free for the taking:

- Celebrate diversity. Every child needs to feel welcome in order to learn. Some schools start by showcasing greetings at the entrance that welcome students in every language represented in the student population.

  Other effective measures include holding multicultural fairs, creating "Human Mosaic" clubs, printing instructions and announcements in appropriate global languages, and honoring the holidays of all cultures.

- Create smaller learning communities. As early as the 1960s, some pioneering schools, such as Evanston Township (Illinois) High School and Topeka (Kansas) West High School, implemented schools-within-a-school organizations to make secondary education more personal and user-friendly.

  Many large urban and suburban schools across the country are now finally embracing the concept as well. For example, the Julia Richman Education Complex in New York City has become a model for high school reform across the country because it is no longer one enormous school. Instead, the sprawling five-story building now houses six small schools, each with its own identity. It is the nation's best model yet for converting a failing large school into a multiplex of successful small schools.

  If your system still operates monolithic learning barns teeming with kids, find ways to break them up or break them down, so they are more manageable for all students.

- Teach higher-level thinking skills to all students. It's a myth that only gifted and talented pupils can benefit from Bloom's taxonomy. Actually, all kids can master and apply these skills with varying levels of sophistication. There is no reason (or excuse) to leave some students out.
- Be sure someone is paying attention to every child. One way is to borrow a page from some community-based youth football programs where coaches "assign" each parent to observe a specific player—other than their own child—on and off the field during every game.

  Later, the parents give the young players positive written feedback on their performance and behavior (even if it's only a comment such as, "You paid close attention and helped by cheering for the team.") It's a strategy to insure that no player goes unnoticed. Can your school make that claim?

  Some school leaders have adapted this approach by directing staff members (including clerical, custodial, and support personnel) to follow the progress of specific students throughout the year. This is an idea you could initiate in your school starting tomorrow morning.

- Don't just require your teachers to read the latest research on learning styles and brain functions. Actually put it to use in every classroom. Train your staff to teach all students in the ways they learn best. That way, you can't leave anyone behind.
- Saturate your school with mentors and role models—particularly for minority male students and adolescent female students. Civic and service clubs and community-minded businesses are fertile grounds for recruiting adult volunteers to work with kids.
- Teach all students the power of goal setting. It can change their lives. You may not be able to develop a formal individual educational plan (IEP) for every child, but every child can set goals and make his or her own plans for self-improvement.
- Recognize that one size doesn't fit all. The best school in the world— even yours—can't be perfect for every student. That's why you should encourage and support alternative, charter, and magnet schools for those students who need them.
- Neutralize bullies and cliques. Too many kids are terrorized by bullies or ostracized by cliques. It happens in all schools. And it keeps some kids from learning.

  One solution that has helped in several schools is to be proactive by introducing a "Respect" curriculum in the early grades (typically second grade).

- Work to have your school designated as an official Peace Site. It's another way to promote tolerance and make all children feel safe, so they can concentrate on learning.
- Apply a gender-fair test to all curriculum, materials, practices, and programs.
- Provide appropriate counseling and support groups for gay and lesbian students.

  New York City has even gone so far as to establish the first U.S. public high school for gay, lesbian, bisexual, and transgender students. The goal of Harvey Milk High School, named after San Francisco's first openly gay city supervisor (who was assassinated in 1978), is to provide students who are often the victims of harassment with a sound education in a safe, secure, and supportive environment.

- Rethink school uniforms. They can help all children feel they fit in. No useful purpose is served by perpetuating a caste system based on designer clothing labels.
- Work to bridge the digital divide. Lend or lease computers to students who can't afford their own. Technology access should be a common denominator, not a divisive factor.
- Reach out to hearing-impaired students. Some schools with sizeable enrollments of hearing-impaired pupils have had success by including "signing" as one of the foreign language offerings open to all students. When hearing kids can communicate better with their hearing-impaired classmates, everyone benefits.
- Find ways to showcase all students. Too often in schools, the same students receive recognition over and over. For a change, try staging a "Battle of the Bands." It often brings attention to a different group of students.

In my alma mater high school, we initiated a "Your Show" talent program open to all kids except those who had already been in a school production or performance of some kind. It became a tradition because it filled a need. Like adults, all kids need their fifteen minutes of fame.

- Establish a free clinic for kids. Work with local health care providers and businesses to establish a walk-in clinic for teens and younger children. Healthy kids show up at school more often and learn more while they are there.
- Position your school as a broker for specialized outside programs. No matter how good your school is, some students (e.g., chronic truants, runaways, and chemically dependent kids) need help beyond the scope of your regular services. So make sure your staff is knowledgeable enough to connect families with the outside help they need.

For example, do your counselors know about the innovative Idaho-based Ascent wilderness intervention program for runaway, rebellious, or recovering teens? They should. And they should also know about countless other local, state, and national resources that can help your students and parents with special needs. Only you can define this responsibility as a legitimate role of the school.

Obviously, none of these examples is earthshaking. But each contributes directly to making things better for individual learners. That's what's important.

If you've ever wondered how to spend your time on what matters most, this is how you do it. Keep doing little things that prevent any child from slipping through the cracks or getting pushed into the corner.

There is a difference between spending your days on the business of helping kids and just filling your days with the busyness of maintaining a bureaucratic system for adults. It's the difference between leading and just holding a place in line until a real leader comes along.

In J. D. Salinger's literary classic, *The Catcher in the Rye,* the angst-ridden hero fantasizes about watching little children play in a field of rye grass at the edge of a cliff. In the fantasy, it is his job to catch any child who is about to fall off. In some ways, this is a metaphor for school leadership. After all, it is your role to watch out for all children and to see that no child "falls off" or gets shoved aside.

In real life, school leaders have the responsibility for seeing that all kids have both access and success in school. That's what makes your job so tough. It's also what makes your job so great. Would you have it any other way?

4 Strong Schools Make a Strong Nation

Education is the chief defense of nations.

Edmund Burke,
British politician, writer, and orator.

Education makes a people easy to lead, but difficult to drive; easy to govern, but impossible to enslave.

Lord Henry Brougham,
in a speech to the British House of Commons

Education stands firmly as the cornerstone of our great nation.

Tom Ridge, Director of Homeland Security

One of the founding fathers' first concerns was to establish a sound educational system. Likewise, the first thing developing nations do today in catching up to the Information Age is to strengthen their educational institutions. People who build nations build schools first. It's what's most important.

That's why literally everyone agrees that good schools are vital for our nation to survive and thrive. Not just some people agree. Not just many people. Not just most people. Everyone agrees! How often does that happen?

People may not concur on what should be taught or how it should be taught. They may not share a common vision of what makes a good school. They especially may not even agree on how much schools should cost. But they all agree that good schools are absolutely essential.

Americans from all walks of life realize that effective schools do more than fill young minds with facts. Schools refine and polish the nation's most precious resource and lay the foundation for a successful future. ("America's future walks through the doors of our schools every day." —Mary Jean LeTendre, American educator.)

Strong schools—

- Pass down the nation's values and heritage from generation to generation.
- Promote a more level playing field for future citizens and open doors to upward mobility.
- Integrate newcomers into the nation's culture. Good schools transform a melting pot into a mosaic.
- Instill self-discipline and standards of excellence in performance.
- Prepare effective leaders (and followers).
- Teach basic life skills to all pupils.
- Develop competent, informed citizens.
- Create an intelligent, skilled workforce.
- Train discerning consumers.
- Prepare effective parents.
- Empower tomorrow's citizens to realize a meaningful, purposeful, and satisfying life.

There are more things schools do, but you get the point. Schools feed the future. (". . . from these halls explodes a nation." —Vance Williams, former assistant principal, Topeka High School.) This makes you part of something big.

Wow! Maybe no one ever explained it to you that way. What you do isn't just important to the nation's welfare; it is imperative.

And this isn't going to change. Good education only begets the need for better education. Ignorance is of value only in a world where it serves some worthwhile purpose. That's not the world we live in. In the real world, a nation never outgrows its need for good schools and good school leaders.

A strong nation requires strong schools. Not just mediocre schools. Not just holding pens for kids. Not just glorified amusement centers with books—but strong schools where real teaching and learning, real work, and real play take place every day. Like your school!?

The power and importance of sound education and robust schools (along with their vulnerability) were most forcibly reinforced for me many years ago when I was first named Social Studies Curriculum Supervisor in a large Midwestern urban school district.

I thought I had snagged a dream job. Dealing with course content, scope and sequence, curriculum guides, and textbook selections instead of rowdy kids, discipline problems, and overprotective parents seemed like a pleasant, no-hassle position. This should be easy and fun, I thought. You guessed it. Wrong again.

The whole episode occurred when the Cold War was at its chilliest. The Russian "Red Menace" was real and many people were genuinely scared. Up and down Main Street, Stalin was viewed as an ogre. After all, communism was out to gobble us up.

Gradually, being responsible for the social studies program (e.g., history, government, and foreign relations) in a relatively conservative community became not so pleasant, easy, or fun anymore.

Like a rising tide, more and more community members began clamoring for the removal of *The Communist Manifesto,* the complete writings of Marx, Engle, and Lenin, and all other books and articles on communism from every library shelf, classroom, or school in the district. Some parents, religious leaders, and political figures began to see "red" everywhere.

My arguments that the best defense against communism was to read and learn about it (knowledge is power) fell on many deaf ears. For certain parents and patrons, every reference or resource with the word "communism" in the title or text became taboo.

McCarthyism came to the Midwest almost overnight. A few self-appointed watchdog groups sprang up and started scrutinizing classroom texts and library collections for any hint of communist blasphemy. Some segments of the community got caught up in a witch-hunt against words.

Some outspoken liberal teachers feared being labeled "pinkos." Our carefully planned social studies curriculum was in jeopardy of being demonized as a Marxist tool. Book banning—even book burning—became a definite possibility. All in the name of God-fearing patriotism.

Fortunately, ardent school supporters and cooler heads prevailed before the worst happened. Faith in the importance of strong schools, in truth, in education, and in freedom of speech proved stronger than fear of communism.

The crisis passed. No books were banned or burned. Our curriculum was saved. My job was saved. More importantly, a whole generation of students was saved from ignorance by censorship. Don't you love it?

I gained some lifelong insights from this experience: (a) Free schools are always fragile, but always necessary as well; (b) in times of fear, it's tempting to kill the messenger—even if the messenger is only a book or a school curriculum; and (c) for freedom's sake, we need to ban fear and bigotry, not books or honest teaching.

Even though I was in charge of the K-12 social studies program at the time, I was the one who learned a basic lesson about what's really important. It bears repeating. A strong nation requires strong schools. Period! ("Only the educated are free." —Epictetus, 2nd century philosopher.)

Of course, there are many ways you and your school can help make ours a stronger, freer, wiser, kinder, healthier society. The first is simply to keep doing what you've been doing—and do it better.

Following are 21 other starter suggestions for enhancing your school's contribution to building a stronger America:

1. Be relentless about basic skills instruction. A dictatorship may not need citizens who can read with comprehension, write with clarity, compute with accuracy, and interpret data correctly; but a democracy does. We're not kidding about competent citizens, skilled workers, discerning consumers, and effective parents.

2. Dare to teach fundamental democratic values as well as facts. Kids need to know that teachers and school leaders stand for something.

3. Model tolerance. School personnel don't just teach what they know; they teach who they are.

4. Maintain high standards and expectations. Low standards only let everyone down; but high expectations can transcend all obstacles. ("We can replace mystery with clarity. Students can replace guess-work with hard work . . . In brief, we can have standards." —Douglas B. Reeves, *Crusade in the Classroom.*)

5. Teach higher-level thinking skills to all students—not just gifted and talented kids. In a democracy, citizens at all levels must reason, make sound decisions, and solve tough problems.

6. Avoid grade inflation and social promotions like the plague. Strong nations are not built on false promises.

7. Make a big deal out of the advantage of diversity. After all, diversity is the lifeblood of a democratic nation.

8. Teach real American history—warts and all. We need citizens who can take the truth, face facts, and build on past mistakes.

9. Teach hands-on citizenship. One of the best examples I know about was an experimental elective junior high summer school course in Topeka, Kansas, called Government-in-Action. Each day, the students would meet at a different municipal, county, state, or federal government site, talk to real elected and career government officials (e.g., legislators,

city council members, air traffic controllers, FBI agents, welfare case workers, and weather forecasters) and ask tough questions about government that most adults would shy away from. The course was a hit with students from all economic and ability levels. Only the questions were different. Could such a course work in your situation?

10. Create intergenerational learning opportunities. All ages can learn from all ages. Senior citizens can benefit from the idealism of youth, while their commitment to responsible, active citizenship can rub off on the young.

11. Break down gender stereotypes. Bring in varied role models and mentors for both sexes. There are no glass ceilings (or any ceilings that limit opportunity) in good schools.

12. Teach citizenship as a basic skill. Don't assume that students will just naturally know how to register to vote, participate in political campaigns, evaluate election ads, or actually cast ballots in primary and general elections. Teach them how. Walk them through the process. Register 18-year-olds at school, and excuse them to vote just as employers allow workers time off to cast their ballots. Preparing good citizens is an important part of your mission.

13. "Stress cooperative learning" as much as competition among students.

14. Make service to the community part of your school's curriculum. Some schools use paid or volunteer coordinators to orchestrate service projects and opportunities for students. St. Louis Park (Minnesota) has gone so far as to initiate an annual Caring Youth Recognition event to honor students who exceed expectations for giving back to the community.

15. Maximize access. All school programs and activities (curricular, extracurricular or social) should be open to all pupils regardless of income or family circumstances (e.g., whenever a fee is charged, confidential waivers or "scholarships" should also be available).

16. Dare to express and display patriotism in school. Kids need to learn that it's OK for adults to be passionate and emotional about our country.

17. Reinforce the partnership between the home and the school. Education in a democracy is a team sport. Where the partnership works, the school succeeds. But where the partnership fails, the school cannot succeed. ("America's future will be determined by the home and the school." —Jane Addams, American social reformer.)

18. Model and nurture "servant leadership." The best leaders are those who serve others best. That's the way it works in a democracy.

19. Solicit and encourage the establishment of scholarships for all kinds of post-high-school education, not just college degree programs. America needs workers with advanced training and sophisticated skills in all fields and occupations.

20. Teach conflict resolution skills (e.g., brainstorming, negotiating, and compromising) to all students. A successful democracy needs citizens who can resolve problems and settle disputes peacefully.

21. And of course—Leave no child behind. ("A child miseducated is a child lost." —John F. Kennedy, U.S. President)

Naturally, the initiatives above are just the tip of the iceberg. If the school is true to its mission, everything it does aids, in some small way, the forging of a stronger union. That's why we have schools.

Today, the nation just may require good school leaders more than ever. This isn't merely a pep talk to pump up educators. It is the cold, harsh reality of a bruising global community.

The truth is that America needs you. It needs you to be the best principal or superintendent you can be. If this sounds like a sermon, it is. Of all that matters for school leaders, this may be what matters most.

5 Schools Are Sacred Places of Hope

A leader is a dealer in hope.

Napoleon Bonaparte, French Emperor

Hope is a risk that must be run.

George Baranas, essayist

. . . and he who has hope has everything.

Arabian proverb

If you have ever sat alone at your desk, in the dark, after the building has finally emptied, listening to the stillness and wondering, "What's it all about?" you can stop wondering. Hope is what it's about.

Hope is simply a one-word mission statement for all schools—especially public schools.

If there were ever an institution that operates on the premise of hope, it is a school. Just as churches provide hope for the hereafter, schools provide hope for the here-and-now.

Without hope, all is lost. With hope, all is possible. Hope is a choice that can become a self-fulfilling prophecy. Hope is a force multiplier. It can transform lives. And more. ("Of all the forces that make for a better world, none is so indispensable, none so powerful as hope." —Charles Sawyer, writer)

Maybe it was the exhilarating rush that accompanies hope that drew you to the profession in the first place. I know that's what did it for me.

By definition, schools are sacred havens of hope—

- Schools embody the hope of a democratic society for a citizenry capable of making the system work.
- They represent the hope of all immigrants for a new life in a new land.
- Schools represent the hope of minorities and children of poverty for something better than street corners, gangs, guns, dope, and early death.
- They represent the hope of all parents who want their children to do better and be better.
- Schools represent the hope of all children who have dreams of happiness and success.

Like home and family, the public schools are a place where, if you go there, they have to take you in—a place where hope never dies.

A school, filled with hope, is better than the tavern "Cheers," where everyone knows your name. It is a place where everyone believes in you and looks out after you. It is a place where possibilities become certainties and miracles happen on a regular basis. Who wouldn't want to work and study in a place like that?

Unfortunately, of course, individuals and institutions can lose hope. When that happens, they give up and stop daring and caring. It's not a pretty sight.

A school without hope ceases to be a school and becomes merely a warehouse, a holding tank or a pass-through staging area for kids. Every child I have ever known deserves much better.

The worst possible scenario is when leaders themselves lose hope. Hopelessness at the top is contagious. It can become epidemic.

I've seen school leaders lose faith, get discouraged, settle for going through the motions and virtually retire on the job. So have you. It's fatal.

You can't have an organization built upon hope when the leader has given up. If the leader loses hope, all lose hope.

Sometimes, others in the organization may try for a while to keep the flame alive within their own domain. As one frustrated administrative assistant once told me, "We try to hunker down, ignore what's going on around us and remain hopeful within our own department; but you can only do that for so long." It takes positive leadership to sustain a hopeful school over the long haul.

When principals or superintendents stop looking forward to each day and are no longer excited about the future, they should give themselves, their families, the school, and countless unnamed students yet to come the gift of getting out.

Some naysayers believe that, sooner or later, all school administrators become burned-out, cynical, and lose faith. I don't believe it. And if you have read this far, you don't either. Hopelessness is never inevitable. I know this, because Luther Crocker taught me that it was true.

It happened while I served as supervisor of social studies for the Topeka (Kansas) Public Schools. During a brainstorming session one day, we decided it was a good time to ignite the social studies faculty with a little outside inspiration. So we initiated a "Visiting Social Studies Teacher" program.

We invited leading schools in the area to nominate their best and brightest social studies instructor to spend a day informing, instructing, and inspiring our teachers. We wanted someone who could demonstrate effective teaching techniques, share success secrets, and spark renewed enthusiasm within our social science department. We chose Luther Crocker.

Mr. Crocker, as his students always called him, was in his 60s and had taught "forever" in the same well-known high school in Kansas City. Over the years, he had observed and participated in the metamorphosis of the school from an upscale school recognized for its high academic achievement into a school with a majority of minority students, a high incidence of poverty, low test scores, high delinquency rates, and all the other problems that accompany such conditions and demographics. On the surface, it was a depressing teaching environment. But as it turns out, depression is in the eye of the beholder.

Luther Crocker was admittedly old, tired, and even a little stooped. He complained of a varied assortment of aches and pains. He told us it was often difficult for him to get out of bed and go to work each morning. He lacked energy and moved slowly.

But as soon as he reached the school grounds and heard the first student say, "Good morning, Mr. Crocker," he felt better.

As he entered the building and more and more students greeted him, he began to stand a little straighter and walk a little taller.

With each greeting, his pace quickened. By the time that he reached his classroom, the adrenalin was flowing and his heart was pumping. He was excited and couldn't wait for the students to show up, so he could get started. It happened every day! That's what hope will do for you.

I don't know how many more years he taught after that, but I'm certain that Luther Crocker never lost his exuberance. I believe there is a little bit of Luther Crocker in all successful teachers and administrators. What do you think?

The truth is that if there is one person who has primary responsibility for keeping hope alive in your school, it's you. ("The role of the leader is to turn on lights. We need to be the most optimistic people in the organization." — Dr. Paul D. Houston, lecturer) But it won't happen by accident, default, or good intentions.

Comedian Bill Cosby once remarked, "Remember the commencement speaker who told you to 'follow your dream'? Well, did anyone ever tell you

you have to wake up first?" Cosby could have been referring to a school's spirit of hopefulness.

Hope is a dream that doesn't become reality by chance. Someone has to wake up and take proactive steps to ignite, inspire, and sustain a sense of hope throughout the organization. Guess who?

Of course, it all starts with attitude. (What doesn't?) As principal or superintendent, your excitement, enthusiasm, and hopefulness can be infectious. But attitude alone is never enough. It takes concrete acts as well.

It's not easy to keep hope alive in any institution—especially in a school confronted with escalating expectations, proliferating regulations, diminishing resources, eroding support, and mounting pressures and problems. But it has to be done; because abandoning hope is not an option—unless you're willing to settle for merely running a cattle pen for kids.

If you're puzzled about how to get started, the following examples illustrate workable ways (some simple, some complex) to help maintain a spirit of optimism in your school no matter how bad times become:

Pay attention to the fourth "R"—RELATIONSHIPS. Interpersonal relationships are the heart of the organization's culture that shapes everyone's attitudes, expectations, and behavior. Relationships are more important than any other single factor in keeping hope alive in the school. Education writers Andy Hargreaves and Michael Fullan *(What's Worth Fighting for Out There)* were right when they said, " . . . it won't be standards, technology, curriculum or new designs for schools that will get at the root of the problem, unless they are accompanied by new relationships between teachers and students."

How people within the organization feel about each other, treat each other, think about each other, talk to each other, and talk about each other determines how hopeful the school can be. People give each other hope. Or take it away.

Some administrators leave relationships to chance. That's not good enough. You can improve the odds of optimism by intentionally nurturing positive relationships at all levels. Can you think of any reason not to?

We all know businesses and schools that boast of being "a family." In many cases, it is either phony hype, wishful thinking, or an illusion. Family members don't manipulate each other, withhold information from each other, or sabotage each other's efforts. If the typical corporate culture is like a family, it's a very dysfunctional one.

But the best organizations, both public and private, really do achieve a family-like feeling of mutual respect, trust, support, and hope. You know schools like that. Yours could be one of them.

For example, I know a group of retired men (teachers and administrators from the same school district) who meet for breakfast every week. Between

20 and 40 "geezers" gather every Wednesday morning without fail to share memories, keep track of each other, and have fun together. It's been going on for almost 20 years.

Any school that builds lasting relationships like that has to be a hopeful place to work and learn. If you build positive relationships, hopefulness will take care of itself.

But how do you do it? It's not that difficult. Simply be honest, fair, open, respectful, friendly, and trustworthy, and treat people the way you want to be treated. (If this sounds like the Golden Rule, it is. More on this later.)

Relationship building may seem too touchy-feely for some, but it works. Every time. Guaranteed. If you are afraid or reluctant to address relationship issues, there just may not be much hope for you or your school.

Create an environment of hope. This means providing lots of second chances, interventions, safety nets, contingency plans, and fallback positions. It's also important to reward effort, pay attention to small gains, and celebrate successes.

One of my mentors made it a point to go to all faculty and parent meetings to share every trophy, award, and recognition the school received. He made it impossible for anyone to ignore or forget what the school had achieved and could achieve again. That's an environment of hope.

Build hope by getting results and refusing to fail. Success is the only surefire way to keep hope alive in any organization. When failure isn't an option, no one ever gives up.

In his shortest speech ever, Winston Churchill urged young people to "never give up, never give up, never give up." This might be a good rallying cry for your school as well.

Barbara Pulliam, former superintendent in St. Louis Park, Minnesota, must take Churchill's advice to heart. When she says she expects every child to learn reading and math skills, she means it. Pulliam doesn't allow any wiggle room for failure.

When she admonished her principals, "I don't want to see any kids you let on the playground or playing video games or going to music class if they're behind in reading or math. . . . Pull kids out and concentrate all day on reading and math if you have to." One principal replied in disbelief, "I didn't know you could do that."

Huh? What was that principal thinking? Of course, you can do that. In fact, if you're a school leader, you have to do whatever it takes to succeed. Anything less and people lose faith and lose hope.

One of the chief differences between a run-of-the-mill manager and a true leader is that a manager thinks accepting failure is being realistic, while a leader thinks it's selling out. Anyone can give up. But no one has to.

Some administrators try to beg off by equivocating that the school cannot succeed with all pupils. Hogwash! Success—and the hope it generates—can occur with all students and in every situation.

Even running a school in the poorest possible environment is no excuse for giving up. Poor urban, inner city, and rural schools can succeed.

If you don't believe it, check our Michael Fullan's *The Moral Imperative of School Leadership*. In this groundbreaking book, Fullan identifies the following characteristics of successful schools that are both "high performance" and "high poverty":

Having high expectations

Sharing leadership

Collaborating

Addressing learning barriers

Staying focused on pupils

Involving families

Identifying interventions

Using assessment to support instruction

Defining special education as a path to success in regular education

Yes, it's true. There can be success (and hope) in any school setting.

If you think you can fail, you're right. You are also well on your way to hopelessness. But if you think you can and will succeed, you are right as well. If you make success mandatory, there will never be a shortage of hope in your school.

Initiate a Distinguished Alumni Award. Recognizing outstanding graduates boosts hope by providing inspirational role models for students, acknowledging and affirming the successful efforts of staff members, and prompting a legacy of community pride.

It's a small investment that can pay big dividends in hope. Best of all, it's easier than you think (see sample criteria).

Sample Alumni Award Criteria

1. Graduated at least 10 years prior to induction.

2. Made a significant contribution to the community and society through service or a distinguished career.

3. Demonstrated those qualities of character, citizenship, and service that form the foundation of a democratic and humane society.

Make time for good news roundups. Every school staff spends a lot of time talking about all the bad stuff affecting the school. If you want to keep hope alive, be sure to give equal time for all the good things that happen.

Set aside time in faculty meetings, student meetings, and assembly programs for young people and adults alike to share their good news.

What better way to promote hope? It's free, it's fun—and it works.

Brighten-up and lighten-up the school. There is little sense of hope in an institution that looks and feels like a dungeon. If that sounds like your school, it may be time to clean-up, paint-up, add student murals, and install better lighting.

When you change the appearance, you can change the personality of the school—and ignite a new spirit of hopefulness at the same time.

Promote health and wellness. When staff members and students feel good and are healthy and full of energy, they just naturally are more optimistic and hopeful. That's why many schools have designated weight and training rooms as after-hours fitness centers for adults and kids, promoted use of the school track as a walking path for all ages during free time, and provided a juice bar in the school cafeteria. How is your school energizing the people in it?

It is difficult to be hopeful when you feel lousy. So it pays for school leaders to do everything possible to keep everyone in the organization feeling fit.

Hire hopeful people. Hopeful people make a hopeful school. You can't afford to hire chronic pessimists, curmudgeons, whiners, crybabies, or naysayers. No school can.

Most schools get the teachers they deserve. Don't settle for "best available" if the best available at the time isn't good enough. Be willing to wait, keep job postings open and start candidate searches all over again until you find employees at all levels who share your positive passion, optimism, and belief in the future. This is hands down the single most important thing you can do to sustain hope within your organization.

Of course, the suggestions above are only teasers. You need to find your own approaches to inspiring and maintaining a spirit of hopefulness in your school.

Thomas Edison was known for saying, "There is a better way to do it. Find it." Good advice. Mr. Edison might have made a good principal or superintendent.

By this time, I'm sure some readers feel this section has made too much fuss over hope. But I don't think so.

I don't want to leave the impression that hope is all it takes to succeed. But I am absolutely certain that you will never succeed without it.

Former New York City Mayor Rudy Giuliani claims that "people follow hope." I believe it is more accurate to say, "people flock to hope." The school systems that radiate the greatest hope for the future become "destination districts" for informed parents.

Hope is a secret weapon that can transform any school into a winner. With proper care, it can blossom and grow anywhere.

Michael Johnson, author of *In the Deep Heart's Core,* may say it best in his moving account of teaching in Mississippi's most poverty-racked region:

> Here in the very core of the Deep South even after atrocity and indignity, the human spirit shakes and stirs and threatens to rise again. Still, hope endures, for one can feel it rising here in the deep heart's core.

It is very easy to forget about or underestimate the power of hope. Don't. Being hopeful and remaining positive about what's possible isn't corny, naive, or Pollyannaish. It's a necessary strategy for survival. Keeping faith in the future gives you a leg up on all the cynics in the profession.

Here's the clincher: Hopefulness is a core trait in every single successful school and school leader I have ever known. I hope that tells you something.

6 Teaching Is the Greatest Profession

Low morale, depressed, feeling unfairly blamed for the ills of society? You must be a teacher.

New York Times, Education Supplement

In a completely rational society, the best of us would aspire to be teachers and the rest of us would settle for something less.

Lee Iacocca, business executive and author

The role of the teachers remains the highest calling of a free people.

Shirley Hufstedler, government official

Not many of you should become teachers, my brothers and sisters, for you know that we who teach will be judged with greater strictness.

Bible, James 3:1

Who are the most important professionals in our society? Doctors? Lawyers? Politicians? Generals? Nuclear Physicists? Principals? Superintendents?—None of the above. Teachers are.

Parents know this. In most homes, the child's teacher is hands down the most important person in the entire community outside of the family.

Of course, there are short-term emergency situations where the family doctor or a plumber may be the next most important person outside the immediate family. Nevertheless, day in and day out, teachers are the most significant professionals to all families with children.

But the significance of teachers goes far beyond child-rearing families. Teachers touch everyone's life. In short, teaching is the greatest profession! The problem is that this is a bad time to be a teacher in America.

Demands are high. Pay is low. Expectations are escalating, while public support is drying up. Even parents are increasingly uninvolved; and litigation is an occupational hazard.

Teachers can't count on anyone to back them up anymore, and their views are frequently ignored by decision makers. At the same time, teachers at all levels and in all fields (especially special education) feel they are slowly dying from strangulation by regulation.

What bothers many educators even more is that pupils are increasingly ill-mannered, disrespectful, and, sometimes, dangerous. (Between 1995 and 1997, 635,000 violent crimes were committed against the nation's public schools by their own students.) It is no secret that many schools have taken on a very rough edge and that maintaining even a modicum of discipline and order is more difficult than ever before.

Worse yet, resources are dwindling, school budgets are growing ever tighter, and teachers everywhere are continuously being asked to do more with less.

To add insult to injury, teacher-bashing has become a national pastime. In some states, governors and other politicians have pointed to teachers as the "bad guys" who are responsible for all the real or perceived ills facing public education today. And it's getting worse. Popular columnist George Will once even described public educators as "a national menace" and "as frightening as any foreign threat." (Does that sound like any teachers you know?)

It is no wonder that few men or minorities are being attracted to the profession and that a severe teacher shortage appears certain in the near future.

Today's teachers are being stretched to the limit—some to the point of abandoning their careers. But most are committed to sticking it out. Why do teachers put up with it?

Teachers aren't stupid or masochistic. The good ones are hanging on because theirs is the most important job they can possibly imagine. They know what others don't: Teaching is the greatest profession because, without it, there would be no other professions.

Besides, the rewards are richer than most outsiders can comprehend. Here are just a few of the powerful reasons why the real pros feel they have to stay, despite the growing accumulation of almost insurmountable problems facing teachers today:

1. Why teach? Because it matters. Not all jobs do.

2. Great teachers make a great nation.

3. Behind all great men and women are the teachers who made them great.

4. Even geniuses need teachers.

5. The founders of all great religions were teachers.

6. Teachers are the nation's unsung heroes. ("The true heroes of our society are not to be found on a movie screen or football field. They are to be found in the classroom." —Elizabeth Dole, U.S. Senator) Police officers, firefighters, and emergency medical personnel save lives, but teachers save the future of civilization. ("Teachers are the soldiers of democracy. Others can defend democracy; but teachers create it." —General Omar Bradley.)

7. Teachers are not only heroes themselves; but they get to see all to tomorrow's heroes before anyone else. Every classroom has at least one future champion. But you never know which student it is. That's why good teachers treat all students like potential superstars.

8. Teachers see magic happen every day. More miracles happen in the classroom than in any church in town. Some laymen don't believe in miracles. That's because they've never taught a child to read. When a child learns, the world becomes a better place. That's why it is difficult for teachers to be pessimistic. They are constantly surrounded by success stories.

9. Teachers have a ringside seat on the enchanted world of childhood. It's what keeps them young. Teachers always know that something important is about to happen. Life is never dull. No two days are alike. Actually, no two hours are alike. Teaching is all about surprises. Every day is filled with them. That's why teaching is more fun than regular jobs.

10. Teachers impact generations of learners. Teachers don't just teach today's students—they teach the teachers who will teach tomorrow's students.

11. Teachers have unforgettable influence. When asked, "Who influenced you most?" few people will identify a stockbroker or an attorney or a

dentist. Most will name a teacher. A good teacher haunts pupils for life. Grown men have been known to sit up straight and put their feet flat on the floor when reminded of a special teacher. You know teachers are influential when the nation's richest and most powerful movers and shakers still refer to former teachers as "Mr.," "Ms.," or "Mrs." Likewise, you know teachers are important when so many people still remember the first one they ever had. Every teacher is a legend to someone.

12. Teaching is one of the few professions in which the practitioners don't compete with each other. Instead, they compete against ignorance, prejudice, apathy, and sloth. And they win every day.

13. Teachers build tomorrow's "fond memories" today.

14. Bartenders, cab drivers, and hairdressers may have heard it all. But teachers heard it first.

15. Unlike most jobs, a teacher's product is never done and never grows obsolete. ("More so than other occupations, teaching is an open-ended activity. In teaching, patients are never stitched, bodies never buried, cases never closed." —Michael Fullan, educator–author)

16. Contrary to George Bernard Shaw's misguided pronouncement, teaching isn't what people do who can't do anything else. It is what people do who can do anything else, but who choose to teach. Today, increasing numbers of men and women are voluntarily leaving other professions to become teachers. For them, teaching isn't a second choice; it's the next level.

17. If you can make it in the classroom, you can make it anywhere. We've found this out everywhere large-scale teacher layoffs have occurred. The unique human and communication skills that good teachers possess are easily transferable to other responsible positions. Former teachers are always prime candidates for employers in all fields.

18. The rewards of teaching don't come just on payday. They come every day. You don't get out of teaching what you put into it. You get more. "The greatest satisfaction of . . . teaching are not found in pay, prestige or promotion; but in psychic rewards." (Michael Fullan, educator-author) A teacher's memorial is in the accomplishment of students.

I'll stop here. Anything further might just be "gilding the lily." Besides, you shouldn't need convincing that teachers make up the greatest profession. If anyone should know it, it is the administrators who work shoulder to shoulder with teachers every day and lead the schools in which they teach.

If you don't know, in your heart of hearts, that teaching is the greatest profession, I'm not sure I would want you running the school my children or grandchildren attend. And I'm certain I wouldn't want to work in your school.

But despite all the undisputable benefits and rewards of teaching, too many teachers are frustrated, depressed, and disillusioned today. They need a boost.

Here's another problem. If teachers are not going to get the lift they need any time soon from government or society in general, where can they get it? You guessed it. From you.

More than better pay, better schools, or better tools, what today's teachers need more than anything else are motivation, inspiration, recognition, affirmation, and encouragement. All teachers need help to

- Feel respected, special, wanted, and worthwhile.
- Restore their resiliency.
- Reverse burnout.
- Resuscitate their pride in the profession.
- Rekindle their passion for teaching.
- Be reminded of why they wanted to teach in the first place.
- Find new meaning in their career.
- Energize their performance.
- Review their commitment.
- Have more fun on the job.
- Get the grit to go on.

Fortunately, these are all things that you, as school leader, can provide. In fact, you are the only one who can provide many of them. And in most cases, they don't cost a cent. Why wouldn't you do this?

If you are interested, following are a few practical examples of ways you can protect, promote, and support your teachers when no one else seems to care:

- Give teachers a break any way you can. Lighten loads. Pass around difficult (and easy) assignments. Grant some slack on onerous deadlines. Insulate staff members from nuisance interruptions. After all, "removing obstacles" is the best definition of school leadership.

- Encourage the community to give teachers a break as well. How about special credit for teachers at local banks, lenient mortgage loans, reduced rates at fitness centers or health clubs, or teacher discounts at bookstores and restaurants?
- Refuse to bad mouth the profession. Even during periods of conflict or in the heat of contentious negotiations, refrain from making disparaging remarks about teachers in general. As a school leader, everything you say should reflect how much you value the special calling of being a teacher.
- In addition to your own behavior, don't tolerate teachers' bad mouthing or undervaluing themselves or their profession. Often, teachers are their own worst enemies.

How often have you heard one of your staff members say, "I'm only a teacher?" What does that do to the image of the profession?

The occupational inferiority complex of teachers was brought home to me again at a reunion of college cronies who had not seen each other for many years. The group included CPAs, a commercial airline pilot, a CIA representative, college professors, an author, and a lifelong junior high teacher. Surprisingly, the teacher expressed some regret that he hadn't done as much with his life as the others.

What his old friends knew that he didn't, was that his life had as much (and probably more) meaning than any of theirs. Over the years, he had touched the lives of literally thousands of students. That's not exactly chopped liver.

It is difficult for society to honor a profession that doesn't honor itself.

Other things you can do to support and promote your teachers:

- Provide your teachers with the best tools available, including interactive "Smart boards" (the next generation of blackboards)
- Encourage teachers to demonstrate the same pride and unity as that exhibited by professional law enforcement and fire fighting personnel (e.g., why don't teachers throughout the city or state gather to attend the funeral and honor one of their own when a teacher dies?).
- Publicize teacher successes and let the community in on what teachers really do every day. Some schools have had success providing virtual classroom tours over the Internet.
- Use testimonials (see examples) to tell the story of the teaching profession. Fortunately, testimonials are easy to obtain (concrete active support is much more difficult).

Sample Testimonials (three of my favorites)

A high priced CEO asked a young teacher, "What do you make?" The teacher replied, "I make kids work harder than they ever thought they could. I make them question . . . criticize . . . write . . . read . . . I make them understand that if you have the brains, then follow your heart . . . You know what I make? I make a difference."

Story reported by Tom Friedman,
New York Times columnist

It was the teachers that made my education challenging and meaningful. . . . I was nurtured, pushed, challenged, brought to task, confronted, tested, redirected, dusted off, put back on track, taught over and over to compromise, to forgive myself, forgive others and teased with cleverness, humor, creativity and compassion. . . .

Margi Youmans, valedictorian, class of 2002,
St. Louis Park (Minnesota) Senior High

If the government ever gives out medals to heroes who infiltrate hostile territory, survive repeated missile attacks, and demonstrate uncommon bravery by turning their backs on the enemy, every teacher in the country should get one. Substitute teachers should get two.

Author unknown

Other ways to elevate your teachers include the following:

- Work for higher teacher salaries. (If anyone questions that teachers are underpaid, look at Silicon Valley in California, where teachers cannot even afford to live in the community they teach in. That's why in California, low-income, affordable housing is commonly referred to as "teacher housing." Ouch!)

Why not give your school board members a copy of *The $100,000 Teacher* written by Brian Crosby, who teaches in suburban Los Angeles? In this attention-grabbing book, the author advocates that the very best teachers (top 5% of the profession) should be paid six figure salaries, while some others should receive pay cuts. Crosby argues that teacher unions protect mediocrity and that there needs to be a real threat of job loss for teachers who fail to meet minimum standards.

Actually, Crosby's salary suggestions may not be as far-fetched as it seems. In 2003, the Governor of Minnesota proposed a "Super Teacher" program that would pay top teachers $100,000 a year to teach in inner city schools. The Governor claims that top talent should be paid dramatically higher and suggests that state businesses help pick up the tab.

On a lesser scale, community members in suburban Hopkins, Minnesota, have already had success by holding "house parties" to raise extra money for teacher salaries.

Whatever works. Anything that you and your community can do to pay teachers closer to what they deserve is the right thing to do.

No doubt, there are countless other ways that principals and superintendents can showcase good teaching and propel it closer to the level of recognition it deserves. After all, the single most powerful determiner of how your teachers feel about themselves, their jobs, and their careers is the way you treat them.

The point is that replenishing today's heroic teachers and giving them the energy to keep trying is everybody's job. But you are getting paid to do it.

The wisest of school leaders know that teachers are the most important professionals in our society. They not only understand it and believe it, they act on it. That's why the second most important professionals in our society are the principals and superintendents who make great teaching possible. Take a bow.

7 Passion Is the Engine That Drives School Leadership

Nothing great in the world has been accomplished without passion.

George Wilhelm Friedrich Hegel,
German philosopher

Think enthusiastically about everything, but especially about your job. If you do so, you'll put a touch of glory in your life. If you love your job with enthusiasm, you'll shake it to pieces.

Norman Vincent Peale,
minister, motivational speaker, and writer

The biggest distinction between effective leaders and also-rans, wannabes or run-of-the-mill managers is passion.

Robert D. Ramsey,
Lead, Follow, or Get Out of the Way

Great school leaders come in all colors, shapes, belt sizes, and IQ scores. But they all have one thing in common: PASSION!

Without exception, the legendary principals and superintendents you know or have heard about are unequivocally passionate about children, public education, and the future.

More than anything else, strong emotion—a passion that won't let up—separates peak performers from pretenders and also-rans. It's true in all organizations, and especially true in schools.

Ordinary or mediocre administrators don't have such intense emotion, or they wouldn't be just average. Even "good" school leaders don't always possess true passion for the job. But all the great ones do. So what is it?

Most dictionaries define *passion* as "a powerful, intense emotion or boundless enthusiasm." Synonyms include

- **Fervor**—a great warmth and intensity of feeling
- **Zeal**—strong, enthusiastic devotion to a cause, ideal, or goal
- **Fire**—a burning passion
- **Ardor**—a fiery intensity of zeal

The great school leaders have these feelings about what they do. Other school leaders don't. It's that simple.

Supreme Court Justice Oliver Wendell Holmes used to describe passion as "fire in the belly." Some educators feel the fire. For others, it may just be heartburn.

Public school leadership may not be a sacred calling, but it comes close. I know that Saint Hubert is the patron saint of math teachers. I don't know if there is a patron saint for principals and superintendents, but there should be. If you are a truly passionate school leader, being an educator is almost a spiritual experience.

Your passion is what you lose sleep over—what you care about most deeply and what you are most committed to. If that happens to be your job, you have a leg up on many of your peers.

Unfortunately, passion is sometimes a rare commodity among school officials. I've known many teachers and administrators who were deeply passionate about their work. But I've also known as many or more who fall short of the mark.

Usually, it is fairly easy to spot those educators who lack real passion for the job. They live for weekends and dread Mondays. They worry about what the school board—or the parents—or the media—might say, instead of listening to what the kids are saying.

They practice "Desktop Management" by spending more time in their office than in classrooms. They like their administrative perks and getting their name in the newspaper.

These are the administrators who complain so much about today's kids that you wonder if they even like their own students.

They prefer harsh penalties, straight lines, and quiet classrooms. They have an unlisted phone number. They wish parents would leave the school alone and let it do its job. And they are counting the days until retirement.

Well, that's enough. You know the type. You've seen plenty of them during your career. You could point fingers and name names (but I know you won't).

The point is that passion announces itself. So does a lack of it. People notice. I recall a school district where teachers once formed a prayer chain to support their dispassionate superintendent's candidacy for a job in another district—not because they wished the superintendent well, but because they wanted a different boss. Like most of us, those teachers preferred passion in their leaders.

Of course, not all school administrators who lack passion are losers. There is no law that says everyone in education must be overcome by a fever of fervor. In many cases, pride, vanity, or a strong work ethic are motivation enough to do a good job. It is entirely possible to have an OK, just fine, or good enough career in school administration without being on fire with passion. But you can't get into the Hall of Fame without it.

Some administrators succeed just by being smart and smooth and good at schmoozing. You know as many examples as I do. Often, they are articulate, charismatic, and driven by ambition to reach the top.

But there is a difference between ambition and passion. Ambition is about the adult. Passion is about the kids. Principals and superintendents can succeed based on their ambition. But it takes real passion to achieve genuine greatness.

Like many emotions, passion may be best understood through example. It is easy to recognize when you see it. If you pay attention, examples are all around you. You may suffer from a serious case of passion for children and learning yourself. (I hope you do.)

In my experience, you are most likely to find examples of intense passion among teachers and administrators—

- Who had trouble in school themselves
- Who came from a family of educators
- Who knew from an early age that they wanted to do something with their life to help others
- Who had to work to pay their own way through college and graduate school
- Who come from immigrant or minority families
- Who choose to work in remote areas
- Who had mentors who were passionate about the profession
- Who could get a more "cushy" job in the suburbs, but remain in the inner city because that's where they are needed most

- Who could make a lot more money in the private sector, but stick with education because it's more important
- Who left the profession for a while to pursue other interests and returned because they missed the children
- Who never thought they would be a teacher, principal, or superintendent, but ended up there because that's where they could do the most good

Of course, role models who are passionate about their work can actually be found in any school—in every school—at all levels of the organization.

If you want specificity, Michael Johnson, who volunteered to teach in the poverty-stricken Mississippi Delta area where he wrote *In the Deep Heart's Core*, is a good example. So is Luther Crocker (remember him?), who survived his school's transition from an upscale school to one serving a poor, minority population, yet still retained his exuberance for teaching well into his 60s.

Closer to home, I'm sure you have countless, firsthand examples from your own experience; but following are four who stand out for me and come readily to mind, because of the inspiration they have brought into my life (They may just inspire you a little as well):

A. B. served many years as superintendent in a variety of small, rural Kansas communities, receiving little recognition and even less pay. But when his superintendency days were over, he wasn't ready to quit.

So he accepted a teaching job in a large city, where he finished out his career. In this new assignment, he was the only staff member to volunteer to teach math and science to the toughest kids in school. He taught nothing but basic and remedial classes, and he loved it.

Despite his age and rough, gruff manner, his at-risk students responded to his teaching and achieved more than anyone expected because they understood that he cared about what happened to them.

During that time, A. B. took a new young teacher under his wing and nurtured the beginner through the awkward, initial years in the profession. He saw potential in the rookie when it was difficult to see. Later, A. B. even offered to personally pay for the young teacher's doctoral studies in education.

I was that rookie. I didn't take his money; but I still owe him a huge debt—which I never got to repay before he was killed by a tornado one summer night in Colorado.

More than anything else, A. B. taught me that it's not about the money; it's about the passion.

George O. was the most senior, most unorthodox, and most enthusiastic teacher in the large high school where he taught for more than 30 years. His energy and excitement were infectious. He was never quiet. He was never still. He never wore down or wound down.

George was passionate about many causes and taught his students to become actively involved in whatever excited them. As a psychology teacher, he didn't follow a textbook, but instead followed the students' curiosity, questions, concerns, and dreams wherever they took them. His teaching style was spontaneous, and his curriculum was life.

George remained the most popular teacher in the school well past the usual age of retirement. In fact, when the state of Minnesota passed a new "Rule of 85" (defining eligibility for teacher retirement as whenever the teacher's age and years of experience totaled 85), George interpreted it in his own way: "Now, I can teach until I'm 85!" he said, and he meant it.

Carol P. was a rising star in the California teaching ranks. She was also a little bit of a rabble-rouser and a leader within the teachers' organization. Until one rainy night, while she was returning from a union meeting, a semi-trailer truck slid into her car.

The accident was horrific. The result was that Carol was to be a quadriplegic for the rest of her life. She could no longer stand nor walk nor completely dress herself nor eat without difficulty. But she could still teach.

After lengthy rehabilitation, Carol returned to her profession. With the help of a retrofitted van, an electric wheelchair, and an aide, she taught special education students until her retirement. She also remained a little bit of a rabble-rouser as a champion for the rights of disabled citizens.

Although younger than I am, Carol taught me (and many others) that courage and passion often go together.

Carl H. was the most recent superintendent I have worked for. He had been raised in a poor family on the Iron Range in northern Minnesota. More than once, his parents received aid from local welfare agencies.

Nevertheless, Carl became educated, eventually earning a doctorate degree in education. His career evolved as well. Carl began as a successful teacher and later served as a principal and an assistant superintendent. Ultimately, he became superintendent of a highly respected suburban school district.

Carl was never ultra-urbane, sophisticated, or polished. He never lost his "range" accent. But his disarming openness, honesty, and sincerity, coupled with his obvious compassion, made him comfortable and accepted in the highest circles within the community.

Late in his career, Carl gave a speech to the local Rotary Club that ignited an entire community to become proactive in meeting the needs of children and youth. As a result, an initiative was born, built around the Search Institute's 40 developmental assets that all kids need to survive and thrive in school and in life.

Named "Children First" (see Chapter 2), the initiative was the first in the nation to rally an entire "village" to be asset-builders for all kids.

Little did Carl realize that his vision would spark a nationwide movement. Today, more than 600 communities throughout the nation and beyond have undertaken similar initiatives.

Even after his retirement, Carl continued to cheerlead and give speeches promoting the Children First concept—always without remuneration.

Carl often confided in me that his effort on behalf of kids was like a calling. He frequently said, "It just seems as if this is what I'm supposed to do."

Carl died prematurely, before he could see the fruition of his work. But the initiative continues—and grows—and spreads. Sometimes, passion can be a legacy.

These real-world role models, and all the others that you and I know about, define passion better than any dictionary ever could.

One interesting observation based on these examples is that, for many educators, the enthusiasm and commitment never stop. The teacher or administrator may retire; but the passion doesn't.

This is true of my first mentor in school administration, now long retired, who continues to train prospective principals and to lobby for better public education. By his own account, he becomes more liberal and caring every year, while most retirees become increasingly conservative. Now that's passion that won't quit. It's no wonder that he continues to inspire me even in our dotage.

It is the same way with a former national-superintendent-of-the-year I know who has published a book designed to help other administrators adjust and adapt to retirement. Here's where the passion comes in: All of the proceeds and profits from the book are donated to a Public School Foundation in the community in which he served as school leader. Even in retirement, he still finds a way to make things better for kids.

With all these examples in mind, the message is worth repeating: All great school leaders—not necessarily all the average principals or the so-so superintendents—but all the truly great school leaders are driven by a passion for what they do. In fact, it is largely the passion that makes them great.

There is a power in passion. It is a secret weapon. Passion gives purpose to your life; it simplifies your work by providing focus and direction, and it multiplies your impact by inspiring others to do and be more than they would otherwise. Passion has the ability to move you and your organization from good to great and beyond.

I've seen average-ability administrators, principals who didn't know what they were doing, and superintendents who acted like "Ned in the third reader" and ran things like it was "amateur night at the Bijou" still manage to mumble, bumble, and bungle their way to success—solely because they cared so much. ("You really can change the world if you care enough." — Marian Wright Edelman, Children's Defense Fund founder)

Never underestimate the power and importance of passion—in yourself or others. Fortunately, the following precepts can help make the most of passionate feelings wherever you find them:

- **Never be embarrassed to let your passion show through.** Passion is contagious; but no one can catch it if they don't know about it. ("Every day you must decide whether to put your contribution out there, or keep it to yourself to avoid upsetting anyone, and get through another day." —Heifitz and Linsky, *Leadership on the Line: Staying Alive Through the Dangers of Leadership.*)
- **Channel passion in the right direction.** ("Part of leadership is harnessing your passions in a way that serves your goals." —Rudy Giuliani, former New York City Mayor.)
- **Rekindle your passion.** Even the hottest fire can go out if left unattended. ("I only fear the 'slowing up' of the engine inside me . . ." — General George S. Patton.) Do whatever it takes to retain your enthusiasm and "love for the game." Revisit your mentor, reread this book, spend more time in classrooms, volunteer to rock babies in a maternity ward— anything that reminds you of what's most important.
- **Temper your passion with reason.** ("If passion drives you, let reason hold the reins." —Ben Franklin) Follow the advice of educator-author, Jonathon Kozol, "Pick battles big enough to matter, small enough to win."
- **Beware of phonies**—especially politicians. Sometimes those who talk the most about their passion for kids and public education have the least. Don't believe all the promises elected officials make or spend the money legislators pledge to grant until the check is in the

mail. Talk is easy. But real passion isn't just a word; it's an action verb.

- **Don't become self-righteous.** Being passionate doesn't make you a better person—only a better school leader. Smug superiority is not a useful leadership trait. It's not necessary that everyone be passionate about what the schools are doing; and you don't have time to try to impose your values on others. It never works anyway.

- **Learn to recognize passion in others.** These are your allies. Not everyone speaks out about their emotions; but their actions often testify to the depths of their feelings. Little things can be the tip-off. For example, educators who care the most are the ones who make it a point to attend the funerals of students or their parents ("Weddings are optional; funerals are mandatory." —Rudy Giuliani, former New York City mayor). The most passionate principals and superintendents are also the ones who visit the Vietnam Memorial when in Washington, DC, to make a "rubbing" of the names of former pupils. Behavior is always a more truthful indicator of deep passion than talk can ever be.

- **Surround yourself with passionate people.** Hire people who share your zeal. It's even OK to bring on board people who are more passionate than you are. They may energize you to new levels of commitment. Unfortunately, real passion doesn't show up on a transcript, resume, or test score. That's why we have interviews. Always ask candidates why they want to be a teacher or administrator. Then watch their eyes and try to look behind their words for their true feelings. Almost everything in our business can be learned, so when you're hiring a teacher or administrator look for the passion first. If it's not there, move on.

Nurturing passion, by these means or any others, is a mark of effective leadership. All of us have to figure out what we hope for and what we want to give our life to. If you can inspire your staff members to make students the focus of their life's passion, you will have the makings of a great school. ("Only passions, great passions, can elevate the soul to great things." —Denis Diderot, writer and philosopher, 1746.)

Your school may not have the biggest budget, the finest facilities, or the latest technologies; but it can be the most caring school on this or any other planet. But if that is going to happen, it must start with a caring leader. That's you. Passion is always the engine that drives superior school leadership.

Enough said. If I have gone on too long about passion, I can't help it. It's a subject I'm most passionate about.

8 What Matters Most Costs the Least

All that is essential is unseen.

> Garrison Keillor, storyteller
> and Public Radio personality

We confuse things with things that matter.

> Noah benShea, poet, scholar,
> and best-selling author

Not everything that counts can be counted.

> Robert Browning, poet

If you need a break, take it now. Then, please pay attention. Don't just gloss over the next few pages, because this is the signature chapter of the entire book.

I can't think of any greater or more important truth for school leaders than the lesson contained in the title above: What matters most costs the least!

If you don't believe this or don't want to, it's time to close the book and toss it aside. You're wasting your time reading any further because we've come to a parting of the ways about what counts most.

The truth is that the hackneyed, old maxim, "The best things in life are free," may sound a little sappy in today's secular, materialistic society; but it's still true—even in your school.

Of course, it's easy to understand why school officials lose sight of this precept. It seems as if every waking hour of every day has to be spent dealing with deficits and scratching for resources. There is never enough money. Or teachers. Or supplies. Or computers.

It's no wonder that administrators, teachers, school board members, and many parents are mad as hell and don't want to take it anymore.

Naturally, it's a disgrace that a democratic society, dependent on an informed citizenry, doesn't adequately support its public schools. It's criminal that the best teachers in the nation make only about 20% or less of what the poorest professional athletes earn.

It's tragic that public school buildings are crumbling all over the country. It's ridiculous that class sizes are too big and school budgets are too small. It's a shame that principals and superintendents earn only a fraction of the salaries paid to comparable managers or CEOs in the private sector. And it's inexcusable that legislatures and congresses giveth with one hand and taketh away with the other.

There is plenty to be angry and frustrated about. But some educators get so caught up in grubbing for money and bellyaching about scarcity that they miss a key point.

Lack of external resources may explain some of the public schools' shortcomings; but it's not an excuse or a get-out-of-jail-free card. The truth is that limited resources can actually facilitate creativity and clarity.

In the real world, even if your school had a budget surplus and the highest per-pupil expenditures in the land, you still wouldn't necessarily have a great school. Limitless resources can create multiple possibilities, but they don't provide any clear direction.

Contrary to what some teacher union leaders might say, the most critical and essential elements of an A+ school have little to do with dollars and cents.

Unfortunately, a few administrators mistake affluence and amenities for substance and significance. Two examples come to mind:

> As soon as S. V. became superintendent of an affluent suburban school district, she immediately remodeled her office, installed a private Jacuzzi, and decorated with expensive furnishings. Soon she was traveling to lots of meetings and conferences—always first class. And she habitually ran up a large monthly expense account.

> Life was good. S. V. was a successful leader. Wrong. Her stewardship and accountability soon began to be questioned. Unfortunately, proper documentation of her expenses was not always available. Rumors spread. Staff morale suffered. Public confidence waned. And the school board bought out her contract.

S. V. had surrounded herself with the trappings of a successful leader. She just forgot to be a good leader. She really didn't grasp what matters most.

Dr. H. was the first superintendent of a newly created intermediate school district. Naturally, he wanted everything to be first class from day one—starting at the top.

He bought the most expensive office furniture available for an elaborately furnished board room, had lavish meals catered in before each board meeting, and provided board members and important visitors with expensive embossed personal notebook binders, designer pens, and other costly memorabilia. His goal was to extend this same sense of ostentatiousness throughout the entire organization.

Dr. H. thought he was creating an image and establishing a "class act." Unfortunately, others thought he was just extravagant, imprudent, and irresponsible. Sooner than he would have wanted, he was replaced. Grand facilities and cosmetic ambiance really didn't matter after all.

Most of the school leaders I know aren't as superficial and foolish as these extreme examples. But some I know do have a distorted perception of what's most important in a school.

You don't have to run a large, well-off, ultramodern school to have a great school. Small schools, poor schools, rural schools, remote schools, one-room schools—any schools can be winning schools ("Living fully does not mean having it all." —Elaine St. James, advocate of simplicity).

As a case in point, I graduated from an urban high school of 2,000 students that boasted of an extensive curriculum, myriad activities, an enormous library, and one-of-a-kind facilities, including a bell tower, an art gallery and, even, a mast (flagpole) from the historic warship "Old Ironsides."

At the same time, my wife graduated from a small high school in a town of 500 residents that didn't even allow dancing at school. Despite the differences, we would be hard pressed to say which one of us received the best education.

Likewise, I have visited a number of "Blue Ribbon" schools recognized by the federal government as National Schools of Excellence. One was in a high-cost, primarily White suburb outside of Chicago. Another was in a low-income section of Albuquerque with a majority of minority pupils.

Yet both of them were chosen as among the very best in the nation. How can that be? Oh yes, greatness isn't a function of size, wealth, or demographics.

Some principals believe they could be superstars if only they could head up a large, new school with all new facilities and adequate funding. You guessed it. They're wrong.

You can't identify good school leaders by the size, age, or wealth of the schools they lead. So how do you spot a real super star? Author Robert Townsend got it right when he wrote

> If people are coming to work excited, if they are making mistakes freely and fearlessly, if they're having fun, if they're concentrating on doing things, rather than preparing reports and going to meetings— then somewhere you have a leader.

I don't see anything in that description that carries a hefty price tag.

Surprisingly (or maybe not), the things that make a truly great school aren't big-ticket items. In fact, they are mostly free, including

Dedication	Personal attention
Cheerleading	Choices
Hope	Risk-taking
Gift of time	Accountability
High expectations	Meaningful dialogue
Second chances	Firm and fair discipline
Challenging assignments	Caring environment
Authentic teaching	Pride in accomplishment
Positive reinforcement	Listening
Excitement for learning	Honest feedback
Respect for individual differences	Rigorous standards
Safety nets	Seriousness of purpose
Straight talk	Commitment to excellence
Praise	Sense of humor
Stretching goals	Real grades for real work

You won't find these things in the school budget, even though they are all essential building blocks for a successful learning organization. They don't cost much. They don't consume many resources. Any school—every school—can afford them. That's good news for all the schools that struggle with limited, finite resources—which is almost every school I've ever heard of.

As further evidence supporting the "matters most/costs least" principle, I submit the following figure that I first used in *Fiscal Fitness for School Administrators* (Corwin Press, 2001, p. 14):

It doesn't cost anything to—
Work smarter.
Be fair.
Ask tougher questions.
Expect students to do their best.
Refuse to inflate grades.
Celebrate successes.
Break down stereotypes.
Establish routines.
Vary activities more often.
Try harder.
Care more.
Support students' dreams.
Believe in kids.
Involve parents more.
Get better organized.
Practice active listening.
Have more fun with kids.

Keep reading to kids at all ages.
Build on strengths.
Help each other more.
Practice amnesty.
Model civility.
Be a stickler for details.
Take students seriously.
Hug kids who need it.
Seek and give feedback.
Treat all kids fairly.
Be the best you can be.
Be honest with students.
Be passionate about teaching.
Smile more.
Always put children first.
Learn from mistakes.

Who says you can't do more with less?

I rest my case. It really is true. The most important components of a "lighthouse" school don't cost big bucks. They are available to every school. They're just not accessed by every school.

Of course, your school needs the things money can buy (e.g., books, buildings, buses, equipment, supplies, technology) to get the job done; but it needs the things that money can't buy even more.

The trick for school leaders is to pay attention to mustering, marshalling, and managing the tools of the trade, without getting conned into believing that's all there is to it.

Today's administrators, including you, have to be prospectors for additional resources more than ever before. But if that's all principals or superintendents do, they're nothing more than glorified fund-raisers. The job is much more than that.

If you spend all your time and energy on the gadgets, gimmicks, and gizmos of education, you risk losing sight of what's really important. ("Things which matter most must never be at the mercy of things which matter least." —Johann Wolfgang Goethe, German poet and scientist.)

The best school leaders balance the tangible (visible) and intangible (invisible) elements of success. Here are ten ways that the best in the business stay grounded by emphasizing the "unseen essentials" that make up a successful school:

Talk about the "unseen essential." ("You lead by voice." —Frances Hasselbein, CEO, Girl Scouts of America.) Use your voice to remind yourself, your staff, students, the school board, and the community of what makes a great school.

Never assume that everyone understands the power and importance of relationships, communication, and the culture of the organization. Effective leadership is a lot about reminding others of what matters most.

Put them in writing. Make values, beliefs, and strategies for helping each other a part of your mission, goals, and strategic plans.

Put them on the agenda. Set aside time at every meeting to consider and discuss feelings, emotions, core values, and the intangible assets of the school.

If all you ever talk about is budgets, deadlines, test scores, reports, and computer programs, people think that these are all that are important.

Teach them. Make sure your programs reflect the unseen essentials that matter most. ("Perhaps education is pointless if it doesn't teach what's important." —Dan Neal, journalist-writer.)

For example, an elementary school in Mound, Minnesota, teaches cooperation, teamwork, and creative problem solving through schoolwide "survival challenges." Teams of students compete in a series of mental and physical contests, such as designing and constructing catapults and then testing them out by seeing which one will propel a projectile the longest distance.

If all your school teaches are facts, you're only running half a school. Life is more than data.

Spending time on them. Make a point to do at least one thing every day to promote or facilitate the intangible curriculum.

Budget for them. The unseen essentials are mostly cost free. But it never hurts to spend a little money on improving relationships, school climate, or the culture of the organization.

Reinforce them. Reward the individuals (at all levels) who best exemplify the unseen essentials that set your school apart.

Some organizations honor employees who save the most money. How about honoring those who make the school a better place to work, live, and learn?

Keep the founders' tales alive. Every organization has stories about the heroes who started it all. Inevitably, these founders' tales are about the values and affirming practices that got the organization off on the right track and need to be preserved to keep it thriving.

Repeating the stories is a painless way to keep everyone focused on what's most important.

Don't get greedy. Resist the temptation to overreach. Some leaders get so caught up in acquiring more (funds, grants, programs, awards) that they ignore what they already have that is most valuable. Former New York Mayor Rudy Giuliani calls it the "Pig Factor." Don't let it be a factor in your administration.

Take stock. Ask yourself and others, "How are we doing? Is what we're doing really important? Will it matter a year from now? Two years? Ten?"

Alcoholics Anonymous challenges its members to "make a searching and fearless moral inventory" of themselves. Would you dare do that with your school? If not, it might be because you already know the outcome; and it's not a pretty sight.

By now, you get the point. The things that matter most in your school don't cost the most. They actually cost the least, so they are easy to lose sight of. It takes discipline and intention to keep them center stage.

I recently heard about an acclaimed composer who was asked, "What makes a musical score or piece great?"

The composer's response was somewhat surprising. He explained it this way,

> The notes are important; but the spaces are even more important. Without spaces, the notes would be just noise. If the spaces are too short, the music sounds jumbled. If the spaces are too long, the piece drags and listeners lose interest. Good musicians pay attention to the notes; but they know it's the spaces that make the music.

It's a little like that in school leadership. Good administrators pay attention to the big budget items that most people think are the critical elements of a sound education, while recognizing in their heart of hearts that it is really the low-cost or no-cost essentials that make or break the school.

There is also something else at work here. Have you ever heard of the "Law of Boomerang Benefit?" It states that what individuals and organizations—including schools—give away will return to them. They get back what they give. In fact, the only way to receive many of the things that count the most is to give them away first.

For example, the only way schools can gain respect is by being respectful of students, parents, and families. Likewise, the more support the school gives to students, the more support it receives from the community.

It works every time. And it gets even better: The gifts are all free to start with. What a deal!

As it turns out, it's not what the school acquires or accumulates that makes it great. It's what the school gives away—such as trust, tolerance, loyalty, and unconditional support—that makes the difference. And here's the best part: As school leader, you get to do the giving.

9 Schools Are Only as Strong as the Community Allows

The school works when the partnership between the home and the school works.

Carl Holmstrom,
former superintendent

If the public were truly to become a partner with public schools in educating our children, we would ultimately see an improvement in student achievement.

Kathy Gardner Chadwick,
Professor of Business and Economics, St. Olaf College

Another part of the job is mobilizing the community to support the work; the school can't do it alone. And the superintendent must find better ways of articulating our story without sounding like we're making excuses.

Carol Johnson,
Superintendent, Memphis, Tennessee

If you have a degree in educational administration, a crackerjack teaching staff, an up-to-date curriculum, a reasonable pupil-teacher ratio, adequate facilities, ample supplies, and enough budget to go around, you have a great school. Right? Maybe not.

What's missing from this picture? The community! Without the public, you're nothing. The school—any school—your school—is only as strong as the community allows it to be.

School administrators can get away with forgetting or overlooking many things. But this isn't one of them. No matter how good you and your staff may be, your success absolutely depends on community acceptance and support. And I'm not just talking about taxes.

Of course, adequate tax support for schools is critical. Unfortunately, many administrators take taxes for granted. Some even wish the community would just hand over the money and leave them alone to spend it. But it doesn't work that way.

The public wants (OK, "demands") value for its investments. ("We are not the bosses of tax payers; they are ours." —T. Coleman Andrews, IRS director, 1955) If you don't deliver, don't count on passing your next levy referendum or bond issue any time soon.

People can get tired of paying higher and higher taxes for education. It's ironic that the scientific name for the American Yew tree, a shrub commonly used in landscaping around Washington, DC, is *Taxus, Taxus*. Many citizens feel their school taxes are like shrubs that keep springing up everywhere and growing bigger and more out of control.

Good leaders don't view taxes as an entitlement; they earn them. But taxes are only part of the story.

The truth is that you need much more from your community than financial support. You and your school need the community's intellectual, moral, emotional, and physical (hands-on) support as well. In addition to the public's cash, you need their heads, hands, and hearts.

If you win over the community's heart, the money will follow. If you don't win over the community's heart, you don't win. Period.

To succeed, your school must count on community members for many things—

- For customers (their kids)
- For helping hands (volunteers)
- For backup (e.g., discipline support)
- For input and ideas
- For what they know about their children that you don't
- For help in improving student achievement (Where parents and other adults are actively engaged with the school, test scores go up. It works every time.)
- For expertise (resource people)

- For business partnerships
- For advice
- For advocacy
- For keeping you honest
- For mentors and role models
- For their energy
- For constructive criticism
- For help to bring about change
- For word-of-mouth publicity and advertising (satisfied parents are the best public relations tool a school can have)
- For validation, and more

With a little thought, I'm sure you could add to this list. But this compilation should be enough to make the message clear: It takes a whole village to run a successful school today.

There may have been a time when the school could pretty much call the shots, operate independently, and still receive unconditional respect and support from the community. There also was a time when dinosaurs roamed the earth. But that's not now.

In this time, in this nation, in your situation, it takes massive public involvement to get the job done. As principal or superintendent, you can't get by just working with students, staff, and parents any more. You have to work with all facets of the community as well.

It may not be in your job description, but a big part of being a school leader today is serving as prospector, recruiter, broker, and coordinator of community resources, services, and involvement.

Naturally, there are many dimensions, of community engagement with the school, including

- Sharing information and data and keeping the community fully informed
- Treating parents and other citizens as valued customers
- Engaging community members in fund-raising activities
- Bringing adults into the school as visitors and volunteers
- Encouraging parent participation in learning projects
- Getting community representatives to sign off on school changes
- Building community consensus on important educational issues
- Collaborating in developing behavior and learning standards
- Forming business partnerships
- Enlisting parents and other community members as lobbyists for school reform
- Involving citizens in strategic planning processes

- Tapping parents for on-site decision making
- Working with the community to take back some of the responsibilities that have been foisted on the school in recent years

The trick for today's school leaders is to engage the immediate and greater community on all of these levels. But how?

Every school has its own pet strategies for engaging the public. Following are some of the best and most interesting ways to gain and sustain community support and involvement. Take your pick. There is no limit per customer:

1. It starts with *communication*. (No surprise there.) That's why when asked by a reporter, "How do you improve the partnership?" Memphis Superintendent Carol Johnson replied, "It requires intentional focus and courageous honest communication." Dr. Johnson is one of those educational leaders who is rarely wrong.

Robert Nordellis, CEO of Home Depot, would agree. He attributes much of his company's success to "over-communicating." This might be a good habit for principals, superintendents, and school boards to acquire as well.

There is simply no way to effectively involve and engage the community without a clear, full, and honest dialogue and exchange of information among all parties. The idea is to be proactive and beat gossip and rumors to the punch.

Effective school leaders reach out to the entire community, target specific audiences when necessary, listen to what the public is saying and tell the public what it wants to know, without lecturing or resorting to educationese (jargon). Sound easy? It is. But it takes a bit of backbone that is sometimes lacking among administrators who are insincere or insecure.

The best schools use every conceivable (and some inconceivable) communication tool, including focus groups, study groups, surveys, polls, large group events (e.g., town meetings), brainstorming sessions, and fishbowl conferences to reach out to and bring in the public. They don't, however, rely too much on newspapers, which today's generation of parents don't read regularly. Instead, they tap into nontraditional outlets (e.g., the Internet, talk radio, cable TV, or virtual reality).

Barbara Pulliam, Superintendent at St. Louis Park, Minnesota, has had success using key community communicators with whom she regularly exchanges information by e-mail.

Whatever works is the best strategy. Try them all. I've never known parents or community members to complain because the school kept them too informed. But I've heard plenty of citizens say they felt "shut out" by the administration and school board. Don't let it happen on your watch.

2. Open up the school. Don't just open the doors; but open up the books and hold open (public-welcome) meetings as well. If you want community support, let the community in—all the way in.

3. Create a positive first impression. That's when many people decide whether or not they are going to become engaged. Pay attention to cleanliness, appearance, curb appeal, and visible signs of pride. Even little things, such as how the receptionist greets people or how phones are answered, can make a big difference.

4. Be honest. Say what you mean. Keep your promises. Most people make their decision about backing the school on the basis of the credibility and reputation of the leader. Until further notice, that's you.

5. Make it easy to get involved. Provide baby-sitters during meetings involving parents. It also pays to serve food and arrange for transportation. Some schools go so far as to hold meetings in the neighborhoods. Technology can also play a role. More and more schools are employing software that allows parents instant Internet access to their child's grades, attendance, discipline record, homework assignments, lunch fund balance, and overdue library books. The more parents know, the more they can help the school help their child succeed.

6. Use what educational writers Michael Fullan and Andy Hargreaves call "Positive Politics" and what President John Adams called "militia diplomacy" to maintain and enhance community support of the school. Fullan and Hargreaves define such nontraditional politics as "diplomacy, honesty, guilelessness, embracing dissent, no shaming or blaming, lobbying for support, building alliances and active listening." Nothing is guaranteed; but "Positive Politics" comes as close to a foolproof approach to greater public involvement as you will find anywhere.

7. Stress courtesy and good manners in all dealings with the public. Politeness is a rare commodity these days. ("If manners were an animal, it would be an endangered species." —Henry C. Rogers, public relations expert) A little civility can go a long way in setting your organization apart from others in the community. It's no secret that people like to get involved where they are treated respectfully.

8. Stalk talent. Keep your antennae out for expertise in the community that you can recruit to help kids learn more or better.

9. Respect and protect family time. Encourage staff members to limit afterschool practices and activities, assign reasonable homework, and coordinate test schedules. If the school demonstrates support and respect for the family, parents are more likely to support and respect the school in return.

10. Encourage the formation and active involvement of booster clubs and alumni associations.

11. Help create a Public School Foundation (see definition) so that interested parties can include contributions to the school as part of their estate planning. This way, community members can continue to support the school even in death, as they did in life.

Definition of a Public School Foundation

A nonprofit, tax-exempt third party to foster education innovation while supplying schools with needed money, equipment, and services donated by citizens and businesses.

---

12. Make the school an integral part of everyday community life for all ages. Common features of a full-service school include:

- Regular classroom instruction for school-age children
- Preschool and day care service
- Afterschool enrichment classes for all ages
- Recreation activities and open gym time and pool time for families
- Summer learning and play activities
- Post office drop-off and pick-up box
- Regular stop for public transportation
- ATM machine
- Return box for library books
- Food shelves for families in need
- Meals on wheels headquarters
- Seasonal tax preparation services
- Satellite "cop shop" (community policing center)
- Congregate dining for senior citizens
- Voter registration and sign-up center for recreation programs

When the school becomes a one-stop shop for community services and activities, public support and involvement just naturally follow.

13. Quantify the monetary value volunteers add to the school (e.g., based on an average of $25 per hour, 200 active volunteers working approximately 4,000 hours during the school year equals $100,000 worth of time.) This can be a powerful incentive for hard-nosed, pragmatic business leaders to get engaged in the school.

14. Always have a wish list and dare to ask for what you need. ("No teacher or administrator ever has to apologize for asking for money for education. If the community offered, the request would never be made." —Noah benShea, poet, scholar and best-selling author.) The community can't fill needs it doesn't know about.

15. Encourage community members to take advantage of the National Principals Hot Line, a once-a-year (usually in April) toll-free phone line and e-mail service in English and Spanish where parents, grandparents, or anyone can get answers to any questions about schools. For some, it can be the first step toward getting more directly involved with their own school.

16. Support a community-wide initiative built around the Minneapolis-based Search Institute's 40 developmental assets that all kids need to survive and thrive in school and in life. When everyone in the community becomes an asset-builder for kids, the school benefits, too. It's already working in over 600 communities nationwide.

17. Use volunteer teachers and college interns to provide hot line or on-line homework help—not for kids, but for their parents. If that doesn't win them over to the school's side, I don't know what will.

18. Sponsor Legislative Tours where parents bring their favorite elected officials on a tour of their child's school. It's a good way to get parents involved with legislators around public education issues and to inform political leaders about school successes, as well as current problems, issues, needs, and challenges.

19. Implement school-based management by establishing building-level site councils (citizens and staff-members) with responsibility for program budgeting and other curriculum, policy, and staffing decision making.

20. Use a "Parent Compact" to spell out parental rights and responsibilities to the school. It works in Romulus, Michigan.

Wow! The list is getting long. But it could be much longer. If you want your school to rise to the top and stay there, you have to do everything you can think of to engage the public on a continuous basis.

I once worked in an older, inner-ring suburb where 87% of the population did not have school-age children; yet voters repeatedly approved excess levy referendums with no sunset provision, which brought in more self-imposed tax money than that enjoyed by any other district in the state. At the same time, many other districts around us failed to pass similar referendums, even if they would only be in effect for a short time.

What makes the difference? The district I served had a history of continuously informing, involving, and engaging the community at all levels. It was simply the way the school system did business. Other districts only turned to the public at crunch time. That's not good enough.

That's why I would never forgive myself if I didn't share this little secret about what matters most for school leaders: The professionals don't set the limits of success for the school. The community does.

If you think you control the destiny of the school, try introducing safe-sex education in a devout Bible-belt community. Or proposing a year-round school in a farming community. Or try to split up a large high school into two, separate smaller ones in a community where the large size of the school has paid off in repeated state football championships. I was there for this last one. It didn't work.

Naomi Judd once said, "Control is a superstition. Control is an illusion." She could have been talking to school leaders like yourself.

There may still be a few school administrators who think they define how good the school will be. But most of these became fossilized long ago. You don't want to be part of an endangered species.

The truth is you work in the only public institution in which the community can directly vote "no" on taxing itself for your purposes. That puts control of the public schools in the hands of the public (which is where it belongs anyway).

You can't develop a successful school in a vacuum today (if you ever could). No school leader can.

What you can do is learn to be a "servant leader" who uses all available social capital (relationships, partnerships, collaboratives, alliances, connections, and networks) to engage the public in helping the school move from good to great.

To succeed today, principals and superintendents have to be more than school leaders; they have to be community leaders.

One of the definitions of *community* in my dictionary is "sharing, participation, and fellowship." Come to think of it, that wouldn't be a bad definition for school leadership as well.

10 When It's Your Own Kid, It's Different

Parents are allowed 20,000 mistakes before they have to apply for refills.

Lawrence Kurner, writer

Deciding to have a child is to desire forever to have your heart rolling around outside your body.

Anonymous

Any fool can criticize, condemn and complain—and most fools do.

Dale Carnegie, motivational writer and speaker

One of the wisest principals I ever knew had an inscription engraved on a little plaque that sat on his desk at all times: "When it's your own kid, it's different." He kept it there to remind him that parents see things differently—often for good reason.

It helped him deal with difficult parents and helped his school develop the strongest home-school partnership in the district. It can help you, too, if you're wise enough to take it to heart.

Many school people today are quick to judge parents. Teachers love to blame parents for unruly students and most other school problems. Some administrators do, too. If you are one of them, you can learn an important life-lesson from the wise principal: Just because parents don't always look at things the same way, doesn't mean they are mean, stupid, wrong, or deserving of disrespect.

If you wonder if condemning parents happens in your school, just listen to what staff members (not just teachers) say about parents in the lounge, during staff meetings, or at the local watering hole after school. It just might be a wake-up call. While you're at it, it might also pay to examine your own comments, biases, and preconceived notions about parents.

Parent-bashing has become so prevalent that John McPherson once featured it in his popular comic strip, "Close to Home." In the comic, McPherson proposed a Report Card for Parents, grading them in such areas as

- Getting student to school on time
- Providing nutritious lunches
- Timely return of permission slips

A few districts have actually attempted issuing such reports. Wouldn't your teachers welcome the opportunity to give out low marks to many of your parents?

The simple truth is that many educators today are overly impatient and critical of parents. It's not surprising, then, that increasing numbers of parents are disillusioned about teachers. Where is this leading us?

Carol Johnson, Superintendent of the Memphis (Tennessee) Public Schools, may describe the growing disconnect between educators and parents best of all:

> In talking with families, I've learned that we tend to see things through different lenses. . . . Some teachers may make assumptions about children from poverty, then those children make assumptions about themselves. Some parents don't think the teachers care; teachers don't believe parents care. . . . Kids need families and schools that see their work as collective.

If you need examples, here's what many teachers—and some administrators—frequently say about the current crop of parents and, in turn, what many parents are saying about today's teachers:

What Teachers Say	*What Parents Say*
Today's parents—	Today's teachers—
Want the school to do their job	Lower standards, water down the
Don't discipline kids at home	curriculum, and inflate grades
Don't respect teachers	Don't control their classrooms

Don't backup school decisions	Don't respect parents
Are too defensive	Expect too much from parents
Question authority	Are too defensive
Take the kids' side	Ignore or deny problems
Won't face hard facts	Whine too much
Try to live through their kids	Look the other way
Don't value education	Care more about test scores than about kids
Don't teach manners and respect at home	Don't value family time
Take school attendance lightly	Have it too easy with summers off
Won't show up	Won't accept accountability
Don't monitor homework	Favor rich kids
Are too quick to sue the school	Assign too much homework
Are afraid of their own kids	Are too bureaucratic
Won't practice tough love	Are afraid of their own students
Don't understand what teachers go through	Protect their own too much
Don't want to pay for good schools	Don't understand what parents go through
The family isn't what it used to be.	Listen to their union more than to parents
	The school isn't what it used to be.

If this kind of backbiting occurs in your school(s) (and it probably does), it is no wonder that the home-school partnership is deteriorating.

Of course, it's easy for educators to underrate and berate parents (and vice versa); but it doesn't help. Blaming and shaming are never viable problem-solving techniques.

Unfortunately, in many schools today, there is too much labeling, generalizing, and stereotyping between teachers and parents, and too many half-truths, urban legends, myths, misunderstandings, and misconceptions on both sides.

This is nasty stuff. As leader of the school, you need to root it out wherever you find it. Finger-pointing has never helped a single child learn any better.

What's needed is a reality check. Students would be better served if both sides stopped whining and bellyaching and showed more understanding, acceptance, and empathy toward each other. It has to start with the school. You can help by reminding your staff of what's right about today's parents:

- Not all parents are crazy, even if it seems that way sometimes. ("About 20% of parents fall into the lunatic fringe." —Edes Gilbert, headmaster, the Spence School)

- Parents send you their very best and most do their best.
- Parents love their kids more than their teachers do.
- Parents know their children better than the teachers do.
- Parents have more access to their children than teachers do.
- Parents are the child's first and most important teachers.
- Parents know all that their children are putting up with in their daily lives better than teachers do.
- Parents have a greater investment in their child's future than the teachers do.
- Parents want the child to succeed as much (or more) than teachers do.
- Parents have more to lose if their child fails than teachers do.
- Parents have to keep living with the results of any mistakes the school makes. Teachers don't.
- Parents are not responsible for all their child's shortcomings. ("Accidents will happen in the best regulated families." —Charles Dickens, *David Copperfield*)
- Parents have no advanced training or degree in parenthood. They didn't take Parenting 101 or pass any qualifying exam. They're pretty much winging it every day.
- Parents never get a vacation. They're on call 24 hours a day.
- Parents can't resign, transfer, or retire. They can't quit or walk away. You never stop being a parent. This is one of those things they don't tell you up front.
- Parents are the only full-time, lifetime advocate each child ever has.
- Parents have the toughest and most important job in all of society. (For what it's worth, teaching may be #2.)

Whew! It's no wonder that parents act unpredictably at times. And it's not just first-time or young parents who act differently, but also experienced parents and parents who are teachers or principals themselves. Even veteran educators are prone to overreact when their own child is involved. Two of the best examples I know about involve a school superintendent and a college football coach.

I once worked with a superintendent who was a consummate professional. He was objective, level headed, fair minded, and caring. He was also an outspoken supporter of the arts. But when his daughter failed to make the cut for the elite high school choir, he almost lost it.

Acting more like a father than a school official, the superintendent openly criticized the music director's decision, verbally attacked the director, called for a reversal, and even threatened to pull rank and overthrow the decision.

Eventually, he reluctantly let the decision stand, but he never quite forgave the music conductor. His animosity continued for years, and the music department never again enjoyed the full support of the superintendent's office.

My colleague was a good leader, but when it was his own kid, it was different.

The second example involved the head football coach at a major university who had no patience for "Monday morning quarterbacks." He didn't like to be second-guessed. He didn't tell other people how to run their businesses, and he didn't appreciate others telling him how to coach football.

But when a referee made what he thought was a bad call against his son in a high school football game, the coach went into a rage. He created an ugly public scene by cursing the referee, questioning the official's credentials, judgment, intelligence, eyesight, and paternity. He even followed the referee off the field after the game to continue his tirade.

Apparently even a college-level professional can behave as immaturely as any other parent.

The point is that, when it comes to their own children, parents don't always behave the way the school wants or expects them too—even when the parents are professional educators themselves. If you only learn one lesson about parenthood during your career, this should be it.

It shouldn't come as any great revelation. All species protect their young from any perceived threat or danger. Why should homo sapiens be any different?

Despite a tendency to be overprotective, parents are still a critical component of the educational equation. You and your school staff cannot succeed without them. No school can.

That's why wise school leaders use every crayon in the box to persuade their staffs to expect, accept, and overlook this natural parental behavior. The goal is to work with parents rather than to criticize or use them as scapegoats. Parents are not the enemy.

If you want to start building greater understanding and empathy between your teachers and parents, there is no fail-safe formula; but the following six steps come as close as you're going to find:

1. Dare to give parents their full say in all matters affecting their children. This includes guaranteeing access to full hearings and a user-friendly appeal process.

2. Encourage teacher home visits. School personnel become much more empathetic when they see the home situation first-hand and interact with parents on the family's home turf.

3. Create opportunities for conversations between parents and teachers. Many of the problems that school staffs have with parents are caused by not speaking directly with parents.

4. Make listening the first step in dealing with parents. Listening diffuses defensiveness. It is always important to communicate, explain, and interpret. But sometimes it's more important to shut up and just listen.

5. Give parents a tabula rasa (clean slate) each year, just as you do their children.

6. When all other criteria are equal, hire teachers who are parents themselves. Teachers who are not parents can be great teachers. But teachers who are parents have an advantage.

When all else fails, reread the title of this section (the inscription on the wise principal's desk). It's an insight that holds true for all parents. It's even true of you.

In fact, it is the key to understanding and working effectively with parents in all situations and at all levels. It's one of the few "one size fits all" principles in education.

I learned long ago not to expect logic from a three-year old, a state legislature while in session, or a parent whose child is troubled, has trouble, or is in trouble.

Since then, my life and career have gone a lot smoother. Now, maybe yours will too. If so, don't thank me. Thank the wise principal.

11 That Pesky Golden Rule Still Works

If there really is a secret to success for school administrators, you won't find it in your favorite graduate program. You'll find it in your family Bible. It's the Golden Rule.

Robert D. Ramsey, *School Leadership A–Z*

The Golden Rule is of no use whatsoever unless you realize that it is your move.

Frank Crane, writer

Show me a school leader who doesn't follow the Golden Rule and I'll show you an administrator who must be misguided, uninformed, or unfit. There. I said it. Too harsh? I don't think so.

After all, the Golden Rule isn't just a religious teaching; it's a hard-nosed, pragmatic principle for success and survival. Treating others as you want to be treated is the key to productive relationships with kids. As principal or superintendent, if you don't get your relationships right, you can't get much else right.

There is nothing more critical in shaping a winning school. Relationships are more important than curriculum, textbooks, technology, buildings, and even money. You just can't have a good school without sound relationships.

That's why the way you treat people in your school has more impact than what you know or anything you say. Kids and adults alike respond to a leader not for who the leader is, but for how the leader makes them feel.

In any organization, productivity is largely the result of the relationship between the leader and the followers. This is especially true in a school that runs entirely on interactions between players.

How those in an organization feel about the organization (and its leader) determines how far they are willing to go, how much they will risk, how hard they will work, and how loyal they will be. Relationships make the organization. In fact, the organization—any organization, including your school— is ultimately just the sum of its relationships.

So if you want to have a peak performing school, it pays to follow the advice of Top Peters and Robert Waterman from *In Search of Excellence*— "Treat people as adults. Treat them as partners; treat them with dignity; treat them with respect." Better yet, do as popular author Richard Carlson suggests—"Treat people as if they are going to die—tonight."

It's that easy. The wimpiest administrator you know could do it. So you have no excuses.

And here's where the Golden Rule comes in. All worthwhile relationships are built on reciprocity. Trust begets trust Respect begets respect. Loyalty is returned in kind. You get what you give. (It's the old reap and sow thing.) It works in your family, with friends, with the school board, and it will work in your school if you let it.

Besides being a religious moral imperative, the Golden Rule works simply because reciprocal behavior is compelling (e.g., if you shout at me, I'll shout back at you). Psychologists have known this for a long time.

Many researchers even believe the human mind is wired with an intuitive inclination toward reciprocal positive social behaviors. Notions of right and wrong or good and bad are probably rooted in our earliest social beginnings and have evolved over ages of social interaction. In short, the Golden Rule may predate the great religions that now teach it.

Anthropology has also long taught us that "one chimpanzee can't be a chimpanzee." Chimps are inherently social creatures and are defined by interacting with and mimicking each other. So are we.

As it turns out, reciprocal behavior is virtually a natural law—a law you can use to propel your school to the top. Why wouldn't you do this?

Of course, there are often some very tempting reasons for all of us to forego that pesky Golden Rule. There are times when treating others as we think they deserve to be treated or as they have mistreated us would be a lot easier and more satisfying. Getting even is fun, and revenge is sweet.

Sometimes, it is inconvenient, uncomfortable, or downright annoying to practice the Golden Rule. But there is always one overreaching reason to stick with it: It works!

I'm sure you have known principals and superintendents who have abused, misused, ignored, demeaned, exploited, harassed, or taken advantage of the people who work for them. How did it work out for them? How long did they last? How are they remembered? Is this the legacy you want to leave? I don't think so.

If you're like me, you've noticed that the truly great leaders don't have to bully people or throw their weight around. They get better results by nurturing, supporting, and empowering others.

But is it really possible to run a modern school—or any complex, highly political organization—strictly by the Golden Rule? You bet! In fact, it may be the only way to run a school successfully today.

It's amazing it has taken this long for so many of us to figure out that how we act toward staff, students, and the public shapes how they react to us. It's so simple.

Of course, that's true of most of the precepts and principles in this book. What matters most is usually pretty simple. It's living by them that is difficult. Sometimes, our sophisticated theories, administrative mystique, and advanced degrees get in the way of recognizing simple truth when we see it.

Ultimately, the real power of the Golden Rule is that it has universal applications. (That's why we find some version of it in virtually all major religions.) This is a principle that works at all levels, in all situations, and with all groups. In your school, it starts with how you relate to staff members (not just teachers, but to everyone on the payroll).

For starters, did you know that, "Unhappy workers don't leave companies—they leave bosses"? That's what leading psychologists Stan Beecham and Michael Gant assert. And they should know. They are also leadership development specialists. Of course, they might as well be talking about schools as about commercial companies.

Wow! That puts a lot of pressure on "bosses" (e.g., CEOs, managers, principals, and superintendents). But handling pressure is what good bosses do best. Fortunately, they have the Golden Rule to help them. So do you. If you treat your employees right, they will treat you right—and the good ones will never want to leave.

If you wonder how it works, I know where you can go for help. Look to the business world. Surprisingly, some CEOs know more about practicing the Golden Rule than many principals and superintendents do.

Robert S. Nugent, CEO of Foodmaster, Inc., is one of them. He explains it this way: "being a good manager of people is mostly not much more than using common sense and the Golden Rule."

Like Nugent, many of the nation's leading executives accept Bob Nelson's observation in the business bestseller, *1001 Ways to Reward Employees:* "How people are treated, inspired and challenged to do their best work determines whether or not you get the most out of them."

It should come as no surprise, then, that some of the best models for "treating people right" can be found in business organizations. Here are three good examples:

Pat Daulton, head of C.I. Title (a title search and mortgage insurance firm in Little Canada, Minnesota) is known for private acts of kindness to employees, as well as for more public gestures such as sending workers home early on nice days or bringing in massage therapists to help workers relieve tension and stress.

Daulton's stated priorities are: "Family first; fun second; and job third." As he explains, "My employees are my partners." Is this the way you think of your staff members?

Across the country in Camarillo, California, Scott Friedman runs another mortgage brokerage firm with similar core principles. Friedman describes his company as a "values-driven corporation run on the values of fairness, respect, and helping people."

As employer, he is known for working with employees to determine fair compensation, supporting family values (e.g., when an employee has to pick up a sick child at school they are encouraged to take care of it immediately and complete work later), and respecting everyone's needs and problems.

Friedman not only applies Golden Rule principles in dealing with employees, clients, and vendors, he institutionalizes these values by putting them on business cards, voice mail messages, and job descriptions. Could this work in your school?

Back in Minnesota, Vern and Helen Olson, owners of Rolico, Inc. (a manufacturer of plastic products) try to treat employees as family members.

They create this sense of family by (a) getting to know employees as individuals; (b) showing interest in workers' lives; (c) setting each employee up for success; (d) keeping an open-door policy that is a reality, not just a slogan; and (e) considering the impact on employees of all company decisions.

It's no wonder that Rolico is described as a "company with a soul." How much soul does your school have?

Of course, none of these businesses is perfect. But they demonstrate what can be achieved with a little Golden Rule management. If the Golden Rule can work this well in the fiercely competitive and sometimes combative world of business, just think what it can do in a school.

Naturally, you can't do exactly the same things businesses do; but you don't have to. What you can do (if you accept this mission) is to figure out what it would take for your school staff to succeed and feel treated fairly. And then, do it.

At St. Louis Park Jr. High in Minnesota, principal Les Bork does it by having his administrative team take turns coming in late and then staying late. This allows each of them an occasional opportunity to eat breakfast with their children, take their kids to school and spend some quality family time that they would miss otherwise. Sounds like the Golden Rule to me.

Patrick Henry High School in Minneapolis does it by borrowing a page from the medical model and treating new teachers as "residents." The resident teachers teach some classes on their own, but also work closely with more experienced teachers to learn new skills and sharpen others at a comfortable pace.

This has to be a lot better than the old approach of handing newcomers their marching orders, showing them their classroom, and abandoning them to sink or swim on their own. (Remember those days? It really wasn't that long ago.)

I read recently that the Australian aborigines take their young people who are coming of age to a great watering hole for 10–14 days, where the elders "dance the secrets" of the tribe for the youth and, through rituals, welcome them as fully participating tribal members. If a primitive tribe takes this much care to introduce beginners to their new roles, can the education profession do less?

At Henry High School, principal Paul McMahon says, "The Resident Teachers are much better trained than those who didn't come through the program." Isn't this the way you wish you had been inducted into the profession?

These examples aren't spectacular; but they illustrate how easy it can be to treat employees right. And best of all, the Golden Rule is mostly free. It doesn't cost anything to do the following:

- Listen. And really hear. Give people your undivided attention when they need it.
- Practice common courtesy and civility.
- Keep your promises.
- Tell everyone what's going on. Be truthful. Open the books.
- Do your share of the dirty work and take your share of the blame for shortcomings.

- Recognize and praise good work.
- Respect people's time on and off the job.
- Buffer employees from "nuisance" intrusions.
- Give staff members latitude to do their job their way.
- Give employees at all levels challenges and opportunities for growth.
- Stand by subordinates who are in trouble or having trouble.

None of these efforts carries a big price tag. But, together, they can return big dividends in heightened excitement, productivity, creativity, and loyalty. Not a bad investment.

Better yet, they work as well with kids as with adults. Even the Golden Rule can be age appropriate. You can't always treat students as you want to be treated as an adult; but you can treat them as you wanted to be treated when you were in school.

Try treating students with the same respect, dignity, honesty, and openness that you show adults. It's not the way your old principal or superintendent probably did it; but it's a great way to run a school—if you like happy kids and excited, successful learners. How does it work? Here are six starting points:

Listen. (Sound familiar?) I know a community that decided its young people needed a place (other than busy streets, sidewalks, or parking lots) to skateboard. Quickly, the powers-that-be began planning a skateboard park that would be private and out-of-the-way so no one would be bothered.

Then, someone decided to ask the kids about it. Surprise. They discovered the adults were planning a park the kids didn't want.

Instead of a secluded place to skateboard, the kids wanted a free, open, visible park near bathrooms and vending machines.

By listening, the city fathers learned that skateboarding is a social event. A successful park isn't just a place for serious skateboarders to enjoy their sport; it's a hangout for spectators as well. As a result, the city didn't waste money on a park no one would use and now has a popular gathering place for skaters, on-lookers, and curious parents.

When kids speak and adults listen, good things happen. It's the Golden Rule in action.

Recognize effort and achievement. Kids crave positive recognition as much as adults. It always pays to praise students often and openly—as long as the praise is authentic. That's why good teachers find creative ways to make recognition meaningful.

Natalie Rasmussen, a winner of the $25,000 Milken Family Foundation Educator's Award for creative teaching, does it by allowing A+ students to sit in her "Fabulous Chair," which she describes as a "hideous, but sacred, classroom prop."

Whatever works. Recognition is in the eyes of the recognized.

Learn the language. Harkening back to the skateboard park example, do you understand the skateboard lingo kids use today? Would you know that an *ollie* is a maneuver to position the board for performing most basic tricks; or that *bail* means an intentional fall; or that a *ripper* is a really good skater; or that *slam* means an intentional wipe-out?

If all this sounds foreign, maybe you should do some homework. Kids need and want to be understood. But it's difficult to communicate when you don't know their language.

Loosen the leash. Everyone appreciates a little freedom. (Just ask your teachers.) You can't let students do everything they want, but you can let them do some things. If you can't let kids leave the grounds for lunch, you may be able to start an "Eat Out Club" by allowing responsible students to eat outside every day. Freedom is an incremental process.

Satisfy students' idealism. Most young people are idealistic and have a need to serve. They want to make a difference and change the world. Why not let them?

Some schools employ a Service Education Coordinator and make community service a part of the curriculum. Others initiate Social Action Clubs to allow students opportunities to get involved in social service projects. If you can satisfy student needs and meet community needs at the same time, that's the Golden Rule at its best.

Prepare students for the real world. That's where they are going to live. If your students come from a "Wasp" suburb, how are you preparing them for life in a diverse society? How about hiring a Diversity Coordinator to create ways to connect students to the real world? Benilde–St. Margaret's High School in Minneapolis does it.

One simple experience the coordinator at Benilde–St. Margaret's promotes is arranging for middle and upper class students to ride a metro bus through low-income neighborhoods in the city. It provides them with a snapshot of a part of the world from which suburban kids are usually insulated. Experiences like this won't change the world, but you have to start somewhere.

If none of these examples fit your school, I'm sure you can think of many others. The point is that students respond to positive treatment just like everyone else. But it doesn't end there.

As well as the Golden Rule works within the school, it works equally well outside the school. As a principal or superintendent, you're making your job much too difficult if you don't apply the Golden Rule to your relations with parents and the public as well. The truth is that if you give everyone in the community straight talk and honest answers while honoring their viewpoints at the same time, you will get what Rodney Dangerfield never gets: Respect!

Contrary to what goes on in many schools, you do the community no favor by hedging on sensitive issues, walking on eggs, or pussyfooting round tough topics. People want the truth—all of it. The truth often hurts, but in the end it really does set you free. That's what you want. And that's what your public wants too.

Of course, practicing the Golden Rule with the public requires understanding what it is that community members want and need.

One of the most creative ways I've heard of for achieving greater mutual understanding is simply to match up staff members with representatives of the school's different constituencies. For example, a staff member might accompany a low-income parent who is applying for government services or shopping with food stamps. In return, the low-income parent might accompany school personnel to various school functions, meetings, conferences, and activities.

There are obvious risks with this approach; but it just might result in enhanced mutual understanding. That's worth the risk.

The purpose of all the examples in this chapter involving staff, students, and the public is merely to nail down that the Golden Rule still works, is working, can work, and should be at work in your school. Many schools have too many rules. A lot of these rules should be eliminated. But this isn't one of them.

You don't have to be deeply religious to be a big believer in the Golden Rule. You just have to pay attention and look around at what is working in the best schools you know of.

Suggesting that you treat others as you would be treated and that they will respond in kind isn't just wishful thinking, Pollyannaish sermonizing or touch-feely psychobabble. It's bread-and-butter survival advice.

The Golden Rule is a guiding precept that's been around for a long time and is good for at least another 2,000 years. There is no recorded instance in which practicing it ever backfired or made things worse.

My minister once shared "10 Rules" (source unknown) that reinforces the powerful message of the Golden Rule:

Rule # 1: Do something good for someone else.

Rules # 2–10: Do it nine more times.

It's too bad that the author is anonymous. Someone should get the credit for succinctly pinpointing the pathway to successful living and leading.

Finally, if you are reading this chapter looking for a fundamental principle of effective leadership or a lasting truth for all school leaders, here it is: *The way—the only way—to become a successful leader is by helping others succeed.* This means treating others as you want to be treated. The Golden Rule is one rule you don't want to break.

12 Someone Has to Be the Grown-Up

When I was a child, I spoke as a child, I understood as a child, I thought as a child; but when I became a man, I put away childish things.

1 Corinthians 13:11

Grownup . . . that is a terribly hard thing to do.

F. Scott Fitzgerald, legendary American author

To be adult is to be alone.

John Rostand, biologist

Every organization needs at least one person who can keep his wits when others don't, resist peer pressure, take the long view, and remain rational and realistic in times of crisis. In short, an adult.

This is especially true in an organization filled with children—some of whom have a license to teach.

Suzette Haden Elgin, author of *The Grandmother Principles,* says it best, "Someone has to be the grown-up." Would a grandmother lie?

Do you remember playing tag as a youngster and hearing the dreaded words, "You're 'It'!" Well, you're about to hear them again.

In your school or school district, someone has to be the adult—not just part of the time, but all the time. Surprise. You get the call. You're "It!"

Acting like a child (sometimes a brat) is tempting. It can also be exhilarating, satisfying, and fun. But it's not leadership. Leadership is for the big kids—the adults.

Many people act like a child once in awhile; but no one wants to put a kid in charge full-time. Even students want the head of their school to be an adult.

In case they didn't teach it in graduate school, this means that your first and foremost challenge as a school leader is to "grow up." It's not quite as easy as you may think. Being a grown-up is a function of experience, growth, and maturity, not age.

If it's been awhile since you were a kid, following are behaviors (actions and attitudes) that most people agree are childish, sophomoric, immature, and definitely unleaderlike:

- Egocentrism. ("My ego is mi amigo.") Self-centered behavior and a "me first" instead of a "me too" attitude.
- Tantrum-throwing—sulking, pouting, and worse.
- Impatience. Seeking instant gratification.
- Name-calling, bullying, gossiping, and rumormongering. Cruelty is a common infantile trait.
- Keeping score and getting even. (What adults know that kids don't is that, "You can't get ahead while you're getting even." —Dick Armey, former majority leader, U.S. House of Representatives.)
- Selfishness—unwillingness to share toys and other things of value.
- Sense of entitlement. Living by the code that Nathan Dungen, author of *Prodigal Sons and Material Girls,* calls the "Teen Commandments" (e.g., Nag and you shall receive, wait not for what you want, and you are entitled to what you want).
- Bearing grudges and playing "Gotcha."
- Overdramatizing. Theatrics. Exaggerating. (What some writers call "Sacramentalizing the mundane.") "Awfulizing." Making life and death matters out of trifles.
- Extravagant bragging and showing off. Excessive "gasconade" (boastfulness).
- Shirking blame. Finger-pointing. Excuse-making. Tattling.
- Flight. Running and hiding.
- Avoidance behavior. Putting off, denying, or ignoring unpleasantness. (As one 10-year-old used to say, "Let's not talk about it.")
- Impulsiveness. Rash behavior.
- Confusing reality and fantasy.
- Sophomore "knowitallism." Thinking you know more than you actually do.
- False sense of indestructibility and immortality.

The list could go on. You probably have some favorites of your own to add. The point is that some behaviors are OK for kids but don't work well for grown-ups.

Unfortunately, childish behavior is not always limited to children. Adults often act this way as well. Some of these adults work in schools—maybe in yours.

Even administrators have been known to engage in immature antics. When this happens, they cease being a leader and start being a liability.

We've all witnessed principals or superintendents who are sullen when they don't get their way, punish subordinates who disagree, hog the spotlight, or act childish in other ways, As a result, they diminish their credibility, embarrass the profession, alienate staff members, and create a drag on the school's chances for success.

If you don't think juvenile behavior by school officials can be a problem, look again at the real-world examples in your own personal experience.

It doesn't take much effort for me to come up with a starter list. I easily (and vividly) remember—

- The principal who routinely hid in a closet to avoid irate parents
- Another principal who crouched down in the back seat of his car to escape unpleasant situations
- The superintendent who used to sneak in and out of the back door to avoid encountering hostile visitors
- The principal who stalked one of his teachers just to make a point
- The assistant superintendent who sued the school district after his boss retired and he was by-passed for the top job. He based his case on the argument that his job description said it was his duty to "serve as superintendent in the absence of the superintendent." Incidentally, he lost.
- The school board member who harassed the athletic director because her daughter didn't get enough playing time
- The principal who insisted his secretary lie for him
- The superintendent who had an expensive private Jacuzzi installed in her office at the same time that the district was suffering from severe budget cuts
- The assistant superintendent who sent principals lengthy voice mail messages boasting about her luxurious winter ski vacation while they remained at home on the job
- The principal who stomped out of a performance review conference with his supervisors because he didn't like what he heard
- The superintendent who routinely "dismissed" cabinet members from meetings as a form of censure

I'm just getting warmed up; but it's too depressing to go on. Anyway, the case is made. School leaders are not immune from making foolish childish mistakes.

It should be no surprise, however, that juvenile behavior by principals or superintendents has never helped a single child learn anything easier, better, or faster. Schools have enough children; what's needed at the top is an adult.

The good news is that there are intentional cautions and precautions that can make it easier to be the grown-up. Here's what some of the best administrators in the business do to avoid making childish choices or acting like an adolescent:

1. Pay attention to your conscience. Child advocate, Marian Wright Edelman, says it better: "Listen to the genuine within you."

2. As backup, get your own "Jiminy Cricket." Ask a close associate (a competent secretary or administrative assistant will do) to serve as your surrogate conscience by reminding you whenever you start slipping into infantile behavior.

3. Stay grounded. Keep in touch with your core values. Reading books like this one can't hurt.

4. Be self-aware and open to feedback. Be coachable.

5. Actually get a coach—a personal life coach to help you keep your priorities straight.

6. Think before you speak—every time!

7. Reread your job description—often. There's nothing in there about being a crybaby or acting immaturely.

8. Don't say anything you wouldn't sign or sign anything you don't understand.

9. Remember the "WWJD" (What Would Jesus Do) buttons? You may not be comfortable with religious references, but it can help to mentally weigh your intended course of action against what you think a respected mentor would do in the same situation. It's like a recovering alcoholic I know who credits his sponsor for his continued sobriety even though he never calls or talks to the sponsor. Instead, he just asks himself what would my sponsor do and then acts accordingly. It works for him. And it might help keep you on track as well.

10. Network with the most mature mentors you can find in and out of the profession.

11. Be reflective. It's a rare trait among busy administrators today. But thinking before you act is never a bad thing.

12. Avoid what Hal Urban, author of *Life's Greatest Lessons,* calls the "EFWIC Disease" (Excuses for Why I Can't). Adults look for a way, not for a way out.

13. Urban also suggests scheduling pain and sacrifice first. Pay now and play later. It's another way to be sure you actually get around to doing the responsible (adult) thing.

14. Take time to make up your mind. Knee-jerk reactions are often childish responses. As Rudy Giuliani, the nation's best-known mayor, advises, "Don't decide before you have to; but be ready to pull the trigger when time is short."

15. Take responsibility for solving your own problems. Don't expect others to do it for you. Learn the lesson of the Native American Hoops Dance. According to tradition, the dancer starts with a handful of wooden hoops, which represent life's many problems. As the tempo increases, he dances in and out of the hoops, slipping them around his arms, neck, and legs until he is entangled in the hoops. The dancer, then calls for help by forming the hoops in the shape of animals, but no help is forthcoming. Finally, the only way to be freed from the hoops is to dance out of them. The symbolism of the dance contains a message for school leaders: The only way to rid yourself of problems is to face them and solve them yourself. It's the adult thing to do.

16. Choose advisors carefully. If you hang out with immature adults it can rub off. It's what business writer John C. Maxwell calls the "Law of the Inner Circle: A leader's potential is determined by those closest to him."

17. Use screening techniques to filter out childish impulses. Try asking yourself "What would mother do?" or "How would this look on TV?"

18. Learn from Zen practitioners. Adopt a special word (e.g., peace or serenity) and repeat it over and over whenever you are tempted to engage in childish reactions or overreactions. It can help keep you focused and on track.

19. Create a "Wall of Gratitude" with photos of all the people who have helped you most. It's a great reminder of what's expected.

20. When all else fails, before you act, always ask yourself, "Is it best for kids?"

Obviously, acting like an adult isn't easy. But it's not like you have a choice. Unlike tag, you can't just touch someone else and make them "It." You're stuck being the grown-up.

Fortunately, it's never too late to grow up. It's OK to listen to your inner child—just don't let him start giving the orders.

One of the well-kept secrets of successful school leadership is contained in the zoological term *neoteny,* which means the retention by adults of youthful qualities (e.g., wonder, curiosity, playfulness).

The trick is to retain a youthful attitude without actually engaging in childish behavior. Leadership is a performing art, and your most important role is simply to act your age.

13 Good Leaders Learn to "K.I.S.S." and Enjoy the Happiness of Subtraction

O holy simplicity.

John Huss, Bohemian religious reformer

Our life is frittered away by details. Simplify, simplify.

Henry David Thoreau, American writer

The ability to simplify means to eliminate the unnecessary so that the necessary can speak.

Hans Hofmann, German-born painter

There is a master key to success with which no man can fail. Its name is simplicity.

Sir Henri Deterding, business observer and writer

Every school leadership situation is different, but they all have one thing in common today: Overload!

The job is becoming too much; there is too much to do and remember. There are just—

Too many rules

Too many regulations

Too many requirements

Too many standards

Too many goals and objectives

Too many pressures

Too many critics

Too many laws

Too many opinions

Too many agendas

Too many bosses

Too many expectations

Jack Welch, legendary former CEO of GE, once observed, "If you're not confused, you don't know what's going on." Most school leaders would say, "Amen." Too many administrators today are "confused" and overwhelmed.

For most of the nation's principals and superintendents, the plate is not just full; it's heaping and overflowing to the point of cracking. Unfortunately, people—even leaders—can crack too.

If none of this sounds familiar, you must have a job in some parallel universe and you are excused from reading this chapter. But for most administrators, overload is a way of life. The good news is that it doesn't have to be that way.

Stop and think a moment. What do reasonable people do when they discover they are doing too much? Obviously, they do less. They cut back, cut down, or cut out. They limit or eliminate. They simplify. Well? What are you waiting for?

Of course, it's easier said than done. Simplifying isn't simple; it's complicated—and difficult. But it's worth it. The reward for simplifying is freeing up your life to have time and energy for doing what's most important.

It's no secret (or is it?) that there is more power in simplicity than in complexity. Simplicity works because it is rooted in common sense.

This makes it a leadership tool that can help school leaders work smarter. Any principal or superintendent would be a fool not to use it. (Fortunately, I'm sure your mother would never raise a fool.)

Psychologists have known for a long time about the "happiness of subtraction." As it turns out, continuously adding on (e.g., more money, more toys or more stuff) doesn't bring happiness. Often, less is better; and happiness lies in removing or reducing distractions and dumping lesser diversions.

Simple organizations run smoother and the simplest solution is usually the best solution. That's why many successful businesses follow the no-frills advice, "K.I.S.S." (Keep It Simple, Stupid).

It works for small businesses like Landy's Bicycle Shop in suburban Boston, which follows only two simple rules: (1) Stop everything you are doing to greet a customer and (2) greet every customer within 20 seconds.

Likewise, it works for huge corporations like Nordstroms, which also sticks with just two rules: (1) Use good judgment and (2) there will be no additional rules. And it can work for you as well. (By the way, how many rules does your school have?)

More courses, more activities, more levels, more layers, more assistants, and more bureaucracy don't make a great school. Doing a few right things and doing them right does.

The key to simplifying school leadership, then, is sticking to basics and doing what matters most. (Reading this book can help.) It often starts by slowing down.

It really is true that "haste makes waste." That's why some hospitals across the country occasionally hand out "S.S.W. Awards" for decisions that are "swift, sure, and wrong." (This might be a good award to initiate in your school.)

Labeling everything urgent, rushing blindly ahead, and working faster don't guarantee better work. Sometimes, it just gets you where you don't want to go quicker.

Joseph Badaracco, author of *Leading Quietly,* describes it best: "Moving at Internet speed is a bad mistake for people going in the wrong direction." According to Badaracco, sometimes it's better, wiser, and faster to exercise restraint, make haste slowly, nudge, coax, and "escalate gradually."

In *Inner Simplicity,* Elaine St. James says, "Hurrying is a habit." It may be a habit you want to break. Doing stuff faster may help you do more; but it doesn't mean you'll be doing the right things.

That's why Law number 17, in John C. Maxwell's *21 Irrefutable Laws of Leadership,* states, "Leaders understand that activity is not necessarily accomplishment." It is a law you can't repeal.

Taking your time allows you to think before you act; to get it right the first time so you don't have to do it over; and to rethink, reframe, recast, and reimage in order to find creative solutions to difficult problems. Slowing down permits you to sort. It's a way to get the most important things done first and fast. (I knew there was a reason the tortoise skunked the hare.)

Best of all, slowing down opens up other possibilities and opportunities to focus, clarify, prioritize, and simplify your life as a school leader. Following are some prime examples worth trying:

Value smallness. Smaller is always simpler and usually better. Small classes are better than larger ones. Those who say that large class size doesn't matter have never taught a kindergarten class of thirty 5-year-olds.

Smaller schools are usually better than huge ones. The smaller the school, the less likely it is that any student will get lost or fall through the cracks.

Even smaller school districts are usually better than large, mega-districts. That's one reason why many large city school systems are not as successful as their smaller suburban and rural counterparts.

I recall several years ago listening to Richard Green recounting horror stories about making the transition from the superintendency in Minneapolis to the chancellorship of the New York City Public Schools.

In New York City, Green doubted if he could even live long enough to visit every school in the system. (Tragically, he didn't.)

In New York City, the custodial union had grown so powerful over time that even principals weren't allowed in their own school without a paid custodian on site.

In New York City, a labyrinth of bureaucracy protected scores of incompetent employees who remained on the public payroll holding down "made-up jobs."

In New York City and in your hometown, size matters. Organizations that are too large are often too complicated, too confusing, and too impersonal.

Of course, school leaders must be good stewards of fiscal resources, including taking advantage of economies of scale. But such economies are only about money. Sometimes, educating children is more important than saving money. Even when it is more expensive, smaller is sometimes better—and always simpler.

Delegate lesser duties and avoid micromanaging. Constantly overseeing or doing other people's work needlessly squanders your time and complicates your life.

Your time is better spent hiring the right people in the first place, so that you don't have to practice "snoopervision" later on.

Trim your goal list. A few goals are manageable; but too many are overwhelming. Some school leaders tackle too much all at once. For example, school administrators are notorious for crowding too many action steps into the first year of their five-year plans. Pacing yourself and spacing your goals are keys to a simpler life.

There is an old saying among legislators, "One good law passed is worth more than a dozen 'half-passed' laws." Who says legislators don't know what they're talking about?

Listen more. It can save you a lot of misunderstandings, misdirections, misfires, false starts, wheel-spinning, and wasted effort. ("Whoever listens most ultimately controls the situation." —Veronique Vienne, writer, editor, and marketing consultant)

Become a little more philosophical. Take things in stride. Not everything has to be done at once. My graduate school advisor, Oscar Haugh, always admonished his protégés, "Don't be a heller, be a what-the-heller." It's still pretty good advice even if you're well past graduate school.

Find a sanctuary in the school. Everyone—even veteran school administrators—need a special place to get away, take time out, regroup, refocus, size things up, see what's really going on, and recapture the big picture. It's called perspective, and it's a prerequisite for a simplified life. I once knew a high school principal who found a haven in the school's wood shop. Where's your sanctuary?

Don't try to know everything. No one can actually know everything that goes on in a busy organization. In fact, it's better if you don't know some things.

Life, as a leader, is simpler and goes better if you hire good people, let them do their job, and rely on them to give you the information you need when you need it.

Only a principal or superintendent who needs to control everything needs to know everything. If that's you, you're never going to have a simple life—You're not going to have a life at all.

Don't try to attend everything. At one point in my career, I was part of a three-member administrative team who opened a new high school. To get the school off to a good start we decided all three of us should attend every school event. It was a big mistake.

Do you know how many games, plays, concerts, debates, field trips, exhibits, and other events go on in a typical high school?

Of course, you do. Literally hundreds. Every month. (And middle and elementary schools aren't much better.)

Amazingly, we got to most activities, but at the cost of planning time, curriculum development time, supervision time, evaluation time, family time—and a good deal of sleep as well. The second year, we implemented a division of labor. Sometimes, none of us showed up. No one noticed the difference.

School leaders don't have to be physically present to support school activities. You can be a spectator and a full-time fan-in-the-stands; or you can be a leader. There's not enough time to do both.

Practice "benign neglect." Try ignoring minor crises that will resolve themselves eventually, can be resolved by others, or will go away with the passage of time anyway. You may be amazed by how much simpler your life can be.

Identify what matters least. It's the flip side of zeroing in on what matters most. You can't avoid "sweating the petty stuff" until you know what the petty stuff is. (See my list below. Yours may be different.)

What Matters Least for School Leaders

1. Worry, regret, and guilt—they take up a lot of time, but accomplish nothing.

2. Titles. What you are called isn't important. What you do is. I've worked for a superintendent who insisted on being called "Dr. —." And I've worked for a boss who wanted to be called "Mike." Mike was the better leader.

3. Perks. Trappings don't make a leader. Results do.

4. Who gets credit. Good leaders give it away.

5. Having to be right all the time. If you think you can do it, you're wrong already.

6. Turf battles. It doesn't make any difference whose territory it is. Just do it.

7. Keeping score and getting even. School leadership is a quest, not a contest.

8. Being the first kid on the block to have something or do something. The smartest school board I ever knew made a decision to settle for being a "7" on a scale of 1–10. That way, they remained close to the cutting edge while letting others work out the kinks first.

9. "Assmosis." "Kissing up" just to curry favor with the superintendent or the school board doesn't work. Doing a knock-their-socks-off job works a lot better.

10. Most standing committees. Nothing deserves its own special committee forever.

11. Meetings held whether they are needed or not.

12. Junk mail—and duplicate reports, which are actually in-house junk mail anyway.

Take time to give clear instructions. That way, you don't have to keep repeating yourself and everyone knows exactly what to do. Fuzzy directions multiply screw-ups that have to be remedied later.

Eliminate clutter. Eliminating clutter from your desk makes it simpler to see what you need to do the job. Eliminating clutter from your mind makes it simpler to see what you need to do next.

Develop a "Personal Work Code" and review it weekly. Include the values and behaviors you want to display. Make it aspirational (stretch yourself) but achievable. It's another way to take personal responsibility for your attitude and the persona you project to others.

Living by your own code (instead of trying to satisfy everyone else's) just makes work simpler and easier every day.

Stop everything and just do it. When things keep piling up and that big project you need to complete keeps getting pushed aside, it pays to dump the minutia temporarily and just do it—finish the larger task once and for all. Lesser tasks can always wait.

I know an elementary teacher who schedules "DEAR" time every day. It stands for "Drop Everything And Read," and it insures that what's most important gets done. It's a strategy that can work in the principal's or super-intendent's office as well as in an elementary classroom.

Outsource pesky duties you never get around to doing. Corporations fre-quently divest themselves of or hire-out excess functions. You can too. It's your job to get things done, not necessarily to do them all yourself.

Just say "No"—to all those things you can't do, don't have time to do, don't want to do, or that someone else can do quicker, better, and easier. You may be astonished by how good it feels once you get the hang of it.

If you need a testimonial, some of the better days of my life occurred when I decided to say "No" and resigned from two foundation boards on which my presence was expected but in which my participation had become perfunctory. The sense of relief was truly one of life's "guilty pleasures."

Tell the truth. It's a lot simpler than tracking a litany of lies and trying to remember who was told what. And as a bonus, you never have to feel guilty again.

Live in the moment and enjoy the process. Life and work seem simpler when you concentrate on the present and take time to appreciate what's going on all around you without obsessing about the future. ("The trip is about the trip, not the destination." —David Jennings, interim superintendent, Minneapolis, Minnesota)

Practice the Serenity Prayer. You don't have to be in recovery or even religious to follow AA's mantra of choice—Grant me the serenity to accept the things I cannot change, courage to change the things I can, and wisdom to know the difference.

Try it. It has worked for millions of people both alcoholics and nonalcoholics. Living this single prayer can simplify and change your life forever, if you let it.

Take a walk. Sometimes in the midst of madness and chaos, the most simple and sensible thing to do is to walk away for a while—and, then, return with renewed clarity of purpose. It worked for Mayor Rudolph Giuliani in the aftermath of 9-11.

Even from this short list of starter suggestions, it is obvious that there is no one easy way to simplify your daily life. It takes will, work, and creativity.

But the alternative is an increasingly congested calendar and a daily glut of administrivia, frustration, disappointment, and thwarted dreams, ending in burnout. That's not leadership. It's lunacy.

This whole book is about simple truths that can make it possible for you to do what matters most. Here's one more. The principles of K.I.S.S. and the happiness of subtraction are lifesaving, career-saving, survival strategies for school leaders. If you want to distinguish yourself as a principal or superintendent, you need to master the art of doing less.

Why? Because simplicity works! It's that simple.

14 You Can't Have Too Much Integrity

Leadership is a potent combination of strategy and character. But if you must be without one, be without strategy.

General Norman Schwarzkopf, U.S. Army

The most essential quality of leadership is not perfection, but credibility.

Rick Warren, author of *The Purpose Driven Life*

When I do good I feel good; and when I do bad I feel bad.

Anonymous old man, quoted by Abraham Lincoln

Ethics is simple, if something stinks, don't do it.

Neil St. Anthony, columnist

"You can't be too rich, too young, too thin, or too blonde." That's what they say it takes to succeed.

Huh? Well, that's what they say it takes to succeed as a California Valley Girl or a Hollywood starlet. Now that I've piqued your interest, the good news for most of us is that this has nothing to do with our business. To succeed in school administration, they should say, "You can't be too honest, too truthful, or too ethical."

The truth is that integrity is the one absolutely essential requirement for effective school leadership. There are many leadership traits that you can ignore, overlook, downplay, fake, compromise, compensate for, or substitute. But integrity isn't one of them. Integrity isn't just a desirable quality for school leaders; it's a professional imperative. I don't know how to make it any stronger or clearer than that.

If I could write these words through a bullhorn or megaphone to command your full attention and come across loud and clear, I would. You just can't have too much integrity!

"Whew," you say. That's easy. Anyone—everyone—can have integrity, can't they? Yes—but—they don't. It's not as easy as it sounds. There's more to it than you may think.

It starts with the definition of integrity. My dictionary says it is "steadfast adherence to a strict moral or ethical code." Can you handle that? Not all of your colleagues can.

Integrity implies the qualities of decency, fairness, honesty, truthfulness, and trustworthiness. It is the antithesis of greed or excessive ambition.

Mark Twain may have said it best:

Have the courage to say no. Have the courage to face the truth. Do the right thing because it is right. These are the major keys to living your life with integrity.

Integrity is unselfish; but it isn't entirely selfless. It simply means thinking enough of yourself to want to be the best that is inside of you.

Unfortunately, some people today—including some men and women in school leadership roles—think this is too stiff an order. Not everyone can be *steadfast* in adhering to a *strict* code. Some don't even think it is necessary or relevant any more.

Most observers agree that, in our society, consumerism and materialism have long since outstripped prudence and frugality. There is obviously a great deal of greed loose in the land.

Cheating and seeing how much we can get away with are rapidly becoming the norm. We see it in business. On Wall Street. In sports. In politics. And, occasionally, in schools.

As society increasingly marginalizes morality, integrity becomes inconvenient and relative in many people's minds. To many, ethics is now situational and right and wrong are no longer clear choices.

Some authors even suggest that ethics should be judged like Olympic diving, so that achievement is measured against difficulty. In that way, you may be deemed ethical enough if you do a little bit of the right thing in the face of a difficult moral dilemma.

More and more, Americans seem to be hedging, wavering, waffling, and weaseling out of tough ethical choices—and expecting credit for trying.

Famed motivational speaker and writer Zig Ziglar disagrees. According to Ziglar, you can't be "relatively honest." You're either honest or you're not. Could anyone with a name like Zig be wrong?

Any degree of dishonesty, lapse in integrity, or failure to follow ethical standards lets others down. If it happens in a school, it's the students, parents, the profession, and the entire community that gets let down. That's unacceptable.

Zig Ziglar is right. Ethics is never obsolete or irrelevant—especially in schools. Principals and superintendents can't get by practicing relative integrity, occasional ethics, or situational morality. You can't be just a little bit right and a little bit rotten and still be a credible school leader.

As society moves toward a vacuum of values, it becomes more, not less, important that the highest officials in public education model unflinching integrity.

Why? For starters, if there were ever an organization that cried out for character-based leadership, principle-centered management, and value-based decision making, it is the public schools—because little children are involved. No matter what else is going on, the nation expects its schools to be virtuous enterprises. That can't happen without principled principals and superintendents.

If that's not enough to convince you of the importance of integrity for school leaders, the following arguments should seal the deal:

- Everything starts with character. Leadership demands believability and credibility. That's why number 6 in John C. Maxwell's *21 Irrefutable Laws of Leadership* is simply, "Trust is the foundation of leadership." If people don't trust or believe you, they won't willingly follow you. You may be able to *run* a school without trust, but you can't *lead* a school without trust.

- Values determine your reputation. As chief administrator of the school, your image and status in the community (as well as your school) ride on public perception of your values. What you stand for determines how many people will stand with you and for how long.

- It has to start somewhere. There has to be a model of moral and ethical leadership among public institutions. If schools aren't a showcase for integrity, where else can it be found?

- Integrity is contagious. One principle-centered leader can infect the entire organization.

- Integrity is essential for individual and organizational health. "Guiltless leadership" (being open and honest) reduces the unhealthy stress of guilt, shame, and fear of being found out. ("You are only as sick as your secrets." —Rick Warren, *The Purpose Driven Life*.)

- The example of the leader is part of the school's informal character education curriculum. It is from observing the behavior of adult authority figures (including teachers and administrators)—not from books—that kids learn the character traits they will exhibit in later life.
- Educational leadership is a sacred trust. If you've read this far in the book, you know what I'm talking about. The responsibility for nurturing the nation's most precious resource (its children and youth) is too profound to be squandered by a lack of individual integrity.

These are some of the compelling reasons why integrity is imperative for principals and superintendents. If you think you can come up with any better reasons why integrity isn't really all that important, you're not only blowing smoke, you're smoking the wrong stuff.

Does all this mean that school leaders are held to a higher standard of ethical conduct than other leaders? You bet. Is that fair? Probably not. But life isn't bound by any law to be fair.

Integrity is part of the fine print in the unwritten contract all school leaders agree to when they sign-on as a principal or superintendent. If you don't want that clause in your contract or you can't live up to it, look into real estate or car sales or some other career. You don't have a job match.

At the end of the day, the only people who resist or resent being held to a higher standard are those who know they can't meet it. Instead of looking for a loophole in the standard, these folks ought to be looking for an exit from the profession. Unfortunately, they don't all take this wise advice.

Of course, no one (not even terminally idealistic education writers) is naive enough to believe that all school administrators are honest and upright. There are scoundrels and scandals in our profession, just as there are in other fields. (Hopefully, not in the same proportion.)

You and I have both known educators who lie, look the other way, exploit and manipulate people, intimidate, discriminate, harass, protect themselves at others' expense, and use their power and authority for personal gain.

I've known administrators who purchased personal items with public monies. I've known others who had adulterous affairs with married staff members (including one principal who actually installed translucent glass in his office windows to conceal his romantic trysts during the school day).

During a lifelong career, you encounter every conceivable kind of misbehavior, misconduct, misdemeanor, and misdoing on the part of school authorities.

But these are rare exceptions. Not all administrators practice squeaky-clean integrity on the job, only the good ones. In my experience, the vast majority are good ones.

Examples of ethical behavior are commonplace in every school, every day. Most school officials consistently do the right thing. But it is not always easy.

It is usually not difficult to figure out what should be done. But sometimes, we just don't want to believe or follow the direction indicated by our moral compass. ("The truth of the matter is that you always know the right thing to do. The hard part is doing it." —General Norman Schwarzkopf.)

The beauty of integrity is that it is seldom played out through grandiose acts of dramatic moral courage, but rather is established through the accumulation of small, everyday ethical choices and actions. That's the way it works in school and in life.

For example, I have a friend (now in his 80s) who spent his entire life working for a major American carmaker and made it a point to always drive his employer's product. Recently, however, he surprised everyone by being the first in the community to drive a hybrid car (gas and electrically driven), which happened to be foreign made. When asked why, he simply replied, "Someone has to start it. It's the right thing for the environment."

It was no big deal. But it represented the kind of unheralded ethical choice that contributes to a reputation for integrity.

In our business, similar examples of everyday ethics occur all the time. It is live-action integrity at work every time you or any principal or superintendent—

- Doesn't lie, steal, cheat, or tolerate those who do
- Takes individual responsibility for a bad call
- Keeps a promise or honors a commitment
- Enforces due process or protects a subordinate from unjust criticism or discipline
- Treats all employees fairly and evaluates staff members objectively
- Assigns reasonable work loads
- Refuses to use the position for personal privilege (If President Harry S. Truman could refuse to use the franking privilege for personal correspondence saying, "Why should tax payers buy my stamps," school leaders can put personal gain aside as well.)
- Reports infractions or violations instead of looking the other way
- Makes full disclosure of financial information
- Lives the mission of the school at all times

OK, enough is enough. I could continue to scroll down example after example, but the point is made.

Integrity is alive and well in public education. Thank goodness. It has to be if the schools are to keep their promise to the nation.

After all this, some readers may feel I'm exaggerating the relationship of ethics to effective leadership. But it's not just me. Here's what a few others (e.g., a president, a prime minister, a motivational speaker, and a business expert) have to say on the subject:

> *. . . the supreme quality of a leader is unquestionably integrity. Without it, no real success is possible, no matter whether it is on a section gang, a football field, in an army or in an office. The first great need, therefore, is integrity. . . .*
>
> Dwight D. Eisenhower, U.S. President

> *If you have integrity, nothing else matters. If you don't have integrity, nothing else matters. That pretty much sums-up ethics.*
>
> Harvey Mackey, motivational speaker

> *Great leaders have a solidity that comes from integrity.*
>
> Margaret Thatcher, British Prime Minister

> *We need authentic leaders, people of the highest integrity, committed to building enduring organizations. We need leaders who have a deep sense of purpose and are true to their core values. We need leaders . . . who recognize the importance of their service to society.*
>
> Bill George, former CEO, Medtronics

Of course, there's more. Much more. But space won't permit it here. If you need further persuading, just look under "Integrity" or "Honesty" or "Trust" in any good book of quotations. The evidence is overwhelming.

True leadership and impeccable integrity go together. You can't have one without the other.

The problem is that integrity and principled leadership don't just happen. They have to be "fed and watered" (cultivated and nurtured) and practiced regularly to remain strong.

But how do you do that? How do you create, develop, or rehearse integrity? There's no step-by-step instruction guide, but the following suggestions can help beef up your ethical IQ (integrity quotient):

1. Intentionally return to basics. Remember what got you where you are. Reading this book or others in Resource B can prime the pump. ("I don't know any society that has been able to continue . . . without acknowledging and reviewing its moral roots." —Margaret Thatcher.)

2. Be open to critical input (constructive criticism). Let others help keep you honest. Even enemies can assist. They won't sugarcoat your shortcomings or settle for telling you only what you want to hear.

3. Talk to those close to you about what matters most. Try holding "Everyday Ethical Dilemma Dinners" with key staff members. Use the time to discuss and thrash out real world ethical issues, such as—
    Is "everybody else is doing it" ever a legitimate excuse?
    Should there be any exceptions to zero tolerance policies?
    Should you share confidential information about a friend's past drug problems with the school board that is considering hiring that person as a principal or superintendent?

Freewheeling discussions on matters of morality can clarify your thinking, renew your commitment to core beliefs, and strengthen your bond with team-members all at the same time.

Introduce your staff to the popular ethics game "Car Town, USA." This interactive simulation game is often used in schools to teach character education. Adults can play, too. The goal is for participants to decide for themselves what's right and wrong, honest or dishonest, ethical or not—it's a playful way to keep ethical behavior at the center of attention.

Find out how others stay grounded and keep their values fresh every morning.

For example, do you know about the Caux Roundtable, a global network of business leaders that has developed a model for ethical business and governmental organizations? The Roundtable has developed a set of "Stakeholder Principles" and, more importantly, a "Self Assessment and Improvement Process" (SAIP) designed to measure the degree to which an organization has institutionalized its ethical values and to target improvement initiatives.

The Caux Roundtable principles are based on the concepts of human dignity (valuing each person as more than a means) and what the Japanese call *kyose* (living and working together for the good of all).

The purpose of the Roundtable is to help organizations create a "corporate conscience." As stated by Roundtable founders, "Leaders who would create a robust organizational conscience must place moral considerations in a position of authority. . . . A failure to institutionalize ethics into decision making at all organizational levels puts the enterprise at risk." No educator could have said it any better.

For more information on the Roundtable, go to http://www.cauxroundtable. com. Check it out. It just may give you some insights you never thought of before.

Use the vision of the organization as a filter for decision making. When you are stuck, ask yourself if you are being motivated by the mission, or by ambition or some other lesser incentive.

You can't go wrong if you stick to the mission, follow your heart, and make the most compassionate choice whenever possible.

Whether you follow these suggestions or not, the goal is to avoid softening your values, settling for partial ethics, or selling out bit by bit.

Not all school leaders can be brilliant or charismatic. But everyone can have integrity. There are no alibis or excuses. You can be as honest as you choose to be.

Another best-kept insider secret for becoming a successful school leader is to become a successful human being first—one who is what organizational management specialist T. L. Stanley calls "an honorable defender of good over bad."

If you are the best person you know how to be, you're well on your way to being the best school leader you can be.

Mae West, America's all-time best bad girl, once said, "Too much of a good thing is wonderful." Knowing Mae, she probably wasn't referring to character, but she could have been. Because it really is true that principals and superintendents can't have too much integrity. Honestly!

15 Common Sense Is Better Than a College Degree

The Grandma Test

Society is always taken by surprise at any new example of common sense.

Ralph Waldo Emerson, American
transcendental writer and philosopher

The three essentials to achieve anything worthwhile are, first, hard work, second, stick-to-it-iveness, third, common sense.

Thomas Edison, American inventor

You would think that intelligent, highly educated professionals such as school leaders would always use everyday common sense, wouldn't you? Well, think again.

Common sense is often a rare commodity in organizations. Schools are no exception. There never seems to be enough good judgment to go around. And unfortunately, principals, superintendents, and other school officials are as prone as anyone to lapses in logic and practical wisdom. If you think otherwise, you're not paying attention.

The truth is that educators do a lot of dumb things. I've done my share. You probably have too.

As I look back, I'm embarrassed by my association with some monumental episodes of illogic and lack of good sense. I've been involved in some doozies.

Early in my career, I was part of a junior high school staff that required final examinations in all classes during the final days of the school year. It kept the pressure on. It kept kids working (and sweating) right up until the final bell. The teachers loved it.

But what the students and parents didn't know was that the tests didn't count. Final grades were recorded prior to the testing period. It was the only way necessary paperwork could be completed in time. Many of the tests were never even graded.

I can't believe I did that. What kind of school lies to its students? How dumb was that?

Years later, I participated in an equally bizarre display of poor judgment. During the rebellious years of the Vietnam era, our local high school had difficulty enforcing its nonsmoking policy.

Kids were smoking everywhere—in restrooms, back hallways, unused classrooms, under bleachers, and in any other available inconspicuous— and sometimes not so inconspicuous—spot throughout the school. Policing became a nightmare. So our crack administrative team decided "if we can't beat 'em, join 'em." We installed a student smoking lounge.

An unused space was converted into a designated smoking area for kids. It quickly became known as "the pit." It was gross, dirty, smelly—and smoky. It was ravished by vandalism and graffiti. Everyone viewed it as a hangout for the toughest kids in school. No adult wanted to go near the place. What were we thinking? We weren't.

Worst of all, we were looking the other way at an illegal activity and creating a major health hazard on site. We should have become the poster school for the tobacco industry and sent home a warning: "Attending school may be hazardous to your health." Where was basic common sense in all this? Nowhere. We blew it. And we weren't the only school to do it.

Naturally, I feel guilty about these outbreaks of poor judgment. The only consolation is that I don't stand alone. Schools everywhere have a track record of foolish acts. I call them "Stupid Educator Tricks."

Here are just a few examples (Look closely, your school is in here somewhere):

- For starters, washing chalkboards. It used to be a widespread practice. Unfortunately, it ruined the blackboards. Anyone—at least, anyone with a modicum of common sense—would have known better. It happened anyway. What can I say?

- Building schools containing deadly asbestos insulation
- Clinging to an agrarian school calendar in an information age society
- Adopting whole language reading programs that don't include phonics
- Punishing whole groups (students or employees) for the infractions of a few
- Using jargon to "communicate" with parents and the public
- Suspending students who would rather stay home anyway
- Inflating grades
- Mistaking the addition of more tests for genuine school reform
- Overmedicating misbehavior
- Adopting complicated grading systems that kids and parents don't understand
- Teaching calculus to teenagers at 7:30 a.m.
- Selling pop and candy bars in school cafeterias
- Paying the best and worst teachers the same (Try explaining that to your friends in the business community.)
- Constructing huge school complexes to house thousands of adolescents in one place (Cost effectiveness isn't always common sense.)
- Locating all of the school's computers in a single lab where they are available only by appointment or on schedule, instead of dispersing them into the classrooms where they can be used as needed (Thankfully, most schools have come to their senses on this issue.)
- Holding summer school in buildings without air conditioning
- Paying floor sweepers more than skilled clerical personnel
- Reducing administrators and public relations staff disproportionately during cutbacks (In tough times, schools need leadership and someone to tell their story more than ever.)
- Making promises (or threats) that can't be kept
- Lowering hiring standards during teacher shortages ("For every time we drop our standards, hold our nose and hire any adult who can fog a mirror, we run the risk of placing a mistake in the classroom for thirty years." —Kati Haycock, Director of the Education Trust)
- Adopting rigid, zero-tolerance policies for weapons in school (How can expelling a kindergartner for possessing a pen knife make good sense?)
- Reducing staff on the basis of seniority (Laying off master teachers while retaining more senior mediocre performers doesn't pass the test of common sense.)
- Banning all vestiges of Christmas or Halloween in schools for little children who don't understand why
- Making a big deal out of spelling bees that give the most practice to the students who need it least, while humiliating pupils who need the most help

- Allowing girls to try out for the boys' wrestling team (Some people think this is reasonable, but it will never make good sense to me.)
- Hanging on to incompetent teachers for 20 or 30 years
- Going on strike (No one wins in a teacher strike, so where is the wisdom of a tactic in which everyone—including innocent children—lose?)

Had enough? The list could go on and on, but it's too painful. The point has been made. School leaders aren't inoculated against dumb acts. Stupidity happens—in schools as in every other area of human existence. But that doesn't make it OK.

Common sense still counts—especially where children are involved. And it won't go out of style any time soon.

As a school leader, you can be smart, smooth, cool, caring, charismatic, committed, creative, and passionate, but it's not enough if you don't possess some basic common sense.

This means facing facts, seeing things as they really are, and telling it like it is. It involves a feel for what's workable, a nose for sheer nonsense, a built-in delusion detector, and a sense of timing.

Without common sense, sooner or later you and your school are going to do something dumb or naive that causes you to lose ground, lose out, or lose your way. Remember "Stupid Educator Tricks?" Common sense is your best—and sometimes your only—stupidity insurance.

So how do you cultivate common sense? One way is to simply apply the "Grandma Test" to all you do or say.

Researchers—especially doctoral candidates in education—are notorious for analyzing the obvious and painstakingly studying the trivial and the ridiculous. This has led Dr. Craig Earl Brock from Penn State to suggest using a *Grandmother's Test* to weigh the worth of potential research projects. Just ask, "Would your grandmother already know this?" If so, it doesn't need further researching.

The same commonsense screening can keep you from making foolish mistakes in your school. Let grandma's logic be your litmus test for decision making. If your grandmother would think a particular course of action is silly, dumb, or off base, it probably is.

In her popular book, *The Grandmother Principles,* Suzette Haden Elgin makes the irrefutable point, "Somebody has to be the grown-up." In your school, that's you.

As leader, you are the one who is supposed to be the grown-up in the organization and to use common sense in managing its affairs. It's an expectation you can't duck, ignore, or fake ("You can't cheat at growing up" —Noah benShea, best-selling author).

So let your grandmother's good sense work for you. It can keep you out of a lot of trouble and set you apart from the many fad-followers in the profession.

Of course, there are other ways to hang on to your common sense when others around you are losing theirs. Following are twenty-five, easy-to-follow guidelines that can keep you grounded and prevent you from overreacting, behaving rashly, falling for foolish scams, or following false prophets. They're grandma-approved and have helped many of your colleagues. It only makes good sense that you should follow them as well:

1. The Golden Rule of common sense: If it seems too good to be true, it probably is.

2. Never sign, buy, or commit to anything you don't fully understand.

3. If you can't frame the issue in simple, newspaper English, back off.

4. Avoid the impulse to be a superhero.

5. If it is unfair, unethical, illegal (or fattening), don't do it.

6. Don't fall into the trap of black and white (either–or thinking.)

7. Recognize when you're in over your head.

8. Avoid panaceas. (They never are.)

9. If it doesn't feel right, don't do it. (We have hunches for a reason.)

10. Remember, timing is everything. If a good idea's time has not yet come, it's not a good idea.

11. Make it a habit to match the penalty to the offense.

12. If you wouldn't want your spouse or parents to know what you're doing, don't do it.

13. Be wary of quick fixes.

14. Don't overcommit, overpromise, overextend, or overspend.

15. Pace yourself. ("Don't fire all of your ammunition at the beginning of the battle" —Joseph Badaracco, Jr., author of *Leading Quietly.*)

16. Expect the unexpected. Anticipate surprises. Ambushes are part of business as usual.

17. Keep as many options open as possible for as long as possible.

18. Proceed with caution. Escalate gradually. Test, probe, and experiment before you fully commit.

19. If it stinks, something's rotten.

20. Listen to what you are saying. If it sounds phony or funny, think again.

21. Have confidence and faith in people, but double-check anyway. (Remember the old admonition, "Trust, but cut the cards.")

22. First impressions are important, but take a second look. Things (especially motives) are not always what they seem.

23. Never rush forward with the one and only answer. Quick answers aren't always right answers. Remember the medical schools that hand out "S.S.W. Awards" (swift, sure, and wrong) for faulty diagnoses.

24. Never be absolutely sure. There is a difference between being confident and being cocky. ("To be uncertain is uncomfortable, but to be certain is ridiculous" —Chinese proverb.)

25. Face each problem as if you were seeing it for the first time. Don't automatically rely on stock or standard responses. Keep a fresh perspective. Start each day with a tabula rasa (clean slate).

Obviously, there is nothing startling or new about these guidelines. They're just—well, you know—common sense.

There are lots of reasons that cause school leaders to make dumb decisions or ill-conceived choices, including—

Lack of experience	Desire to please
Naiveté	Timidity
Ego	Stubbornness
Blind ambition	Wishful thinking
Bad advice	Need for approval
Fear	Herd instinct
Not paying attention	Misreading situations
Rush to judgment	Denial
Tunnel vision	Biased thinking

Likewise, there are many factors that can go into better decision making, including—

Past experience	Research findings
Trend spotting	Expert opinion
Prevailing practice	Data analysis
Precedent	Intuition
Valid input	Basic values

What's missing from both lists? Common sense!

If you want to lead your school, making fewer embarrassing miscalculations and more bull's-eye calls, don't leave it off your list.

One of the timeless truths of our profession is that common sense is uncommon. A second truth is that it doesn't have to be that way.

Successful leaders in all fields value simple good judgment. Today, we often call it "street smarts." It's worth more than a college degree. In fact, it's a survival tool for all ages.

Take time every time to weigh practical considerations, apply reality checks, and buttress judgment with old-fashioned good sense. You'll be glad you did. So will your grandma.

16 Sometimes Kids Need Candy More Than Milk

Here's an anecdote that has stuck with me for many years—

> After herding her band of babies through the grocery store checkout lane, a frazzled welfare mother purchased a number of candy bars and paid for them with food stamps.
>
> Behind her in line, a disapproving middle class matron snorted, "You shouldn't waste your food stamps on candy. Your babies need milk."
>
> Exasperated, the welfare mom retorted, "I'm sorry, but sometimes children need candy more than milk," and proceeded to leave with her brood of infants in tow.

I used to think this little story was slightly exaggerated and mildly amusing. But now, I'm convinced it is just true enough and profound enough to be included in a book about what counts most for school leaders. How did that happen?

Kids may need candy as much as or more than milk? Huh? This doesn't exactly sound like a timeless lesson that all good school leaders should internalize and incorporate, but it is.

The candy and milk thing really is true. Always has been. Always will be. But some educators—you probably know a few of them—ignore it, deny it, or insist on acting as if they don't believe it.

Unfortunately, these naysayers are clueless about one of the dirty little secrets of education—it has to be sweetened with a little fun now and then to be effective. A spoonful of sugar really works.

It is in the nature of children to crave a little amusement, excitement, entertainment, diversion, and old-fashioned fun along with the hard work of learning. Otherwise, they get bored, cranky, restless, and rebellious. (Their teachers are the same way.)

No matter how good teachers and administrators are or how many college degrees they have, they can't repeal the law of gravity or change the nature of kids. To try is a self-defeating exercise in futility. But that doesn't stop some of your peers in the profession from making the effort.

We all know hard-nosed teachers who run a humorless classroom and think that any sign of silliness or fun trivializes the serious intent of schooling. They are well meaning, but they make their job much harder than it should be.

A popular professor of elementary education once explained it to me this way: A classroom that is always noisy may be out of control. A classroom that is noisy sometimes and quiet at others is probably a productive one. But a classroom that is always still has a teacher who doesn't understand kids.

Of course, it's not just teachers who can be uptight, rule-bound or overly image-conscious. We've all worked for or with a few administrators who are the same way.

For example, I know of one newly hired superintendent in a Midwestern city who alienated teachers and parents alike even before his real first day on the job by announcing in advance that "there will be no classroom parties next year."

I'm not sure he ever fully recovered from this public relations disaster. How does a person become a superintendent without knowing what every welfare mom knows—kids need a little candy once in a while.

The trouble with most no-frills, no-fun educators is that they take themselves much too seriously. They're missing the point. Education is too serious to be taken seriously all the time. If this isn't somebody's law, it should be.

Despite all the recent hype about standards, test scores, and accountability, schools can't be all hard work, homework, and busywork. There needs to be room for fun and laughter as well. ("All work and no play . . ."—well, you know how that turns out.) In the classic movie *Zorba the Greek*, Zorba says, "Man needs a little madness." So do kids!

If educators don't make school fun, children will make their own fun. That's not always a good thing.

Of course, schools have to take care of first things first—reading, writing, and computation. But if that's all we do we don't need five days a week, nine months a year for thirteen years. There's time for a lot more.

Good schools use some of this time to lighten up, let kids be kids, and have fun with learning. For some students this is the best part of their education. For all students, there are times when the dessert is the best part of the meal.

Schools should be fun for kids. If yours isn't, you're doing something wrong. There is intrinsic joy in teaching and learning—unless and until the adults involved (that could be you and your staff) stifle it and make learning too stuffy and stodgy for children to enjoy. When students ask, "Are we having fun yet?" it's not just a rhetorical question. If education ceases to be fun (at least occasionally) kids won't want any.

I remember hearing a few years ago about a high school physics teacher who understood this principle as well as anyone. Instead of relying on boring texts and dry lectures, he used Disney-type theme park rides as a laboratory where students learned, tested, and validated scientific laws, while getting some thrills and having fun at the same time.

Now here is a guy who has mastered the idea of milk and candy. We need more teachers like that. You need more teachers like that.

It's the leader who sets the tone for the entire organization and creates an environment where joy and learning flourish together. As head of the school, you have to lighten up before everyone else feels free to do the same. The best school leaders don't just give permission for fun to occur in the classroom, they insist on it.

In the business world, veteran columnist Dale Dauten (the "Corporate Curmudgeon") writes about "laughing warriors"—business leaders who are driven, competitive, effective, and successful, but in a "light-hearted and appealing way." This might be a good model for school leaders as well.

What the laughing warriors know that some school administrators don't is that everyone (including kids) needs some fun and balance in their life, that you don't always have to be serious to earn respect, and that having fun makes the workplace (school) better for everyone.

Of course, a good thing can be carried to extremes. Examples include David Moore, CEO of his own venture-capital firm, who is one of several successful top executives who actually have done stand-up comedy in clubs on weekends.

School leaders don't have to become comedians, but they do need to—

- Have a sense of humor
- Be fun-loving
- Be able to spot absurdity when they see it
- Encourage playfulness
- Value laughter
- Enjoy seeing others enjoying themselves
- Be capable of laughing at themselves

How do you rate on the laughing warrior scale? It's important, because a fun-loving leader makes a fun-loving school. And where kids have fun in school, they work harder and learn more.

That's why many school districts have adopted the popular business book *Fish: A Remarkable Way to Boost Morale and Improve Results* as required reading for principals. In this modern day classic, the authors use the real-world example of the phenomenally successful Pike Street Fish Market in Seattle to reveal the power of lightening up on the job and making each day memorable for everyone. According to *Fish*, "What's fun, gets done."

Obviously, this book isn't just a must-read guide for business leaders. It contains a not-to-be-forgotten lesson for educators as well. If there isn't anything "fishy" going on in every one of your classrooms every day, there should be.

This is essentially the same idea that Ron Clark, Disney 2001 Teacher of the Year, writes about in his popular best seller, *The Essential "55": Rules for Discovering the Successful Student in Every Child.* At the end of the book, Clark stresses the importance of creating memorable (special) moments and adding magic to the lives of every child. As examples, Clark cites specific experiences from his own work with kids, such as visiting the White House and obtaining front row seats for a Broadway production.

Naturally, all learning experiences should be important; but the special moments Clark talks about are crucibles that can define or change the lives of students forever. They are the sweetener that all children need now and then as part of their overall educational diet.

I believe Ron Clark knows what he's talking about. We all can identify examples from our own lives and careers. Here are two brief vignettes depicting special crucibles from my own experience:

When my daughter was in junior high school, a veteran teacher who also advised the camera club sponsored a student photo contest. The first prize was a solo flight over the city with the teacher, who was a licensed pilot.

My daughter entered and won. Naturally, she was excited about winning and enjoyed the plane ride. But it didn't end there.

With renewed interest, our daughter pursued more photographic experience in high school and ultimately became photographer for the school yearbook. Later, she attended the Colorado Institute of Art, majoring in photography.

Since graduation, she has worked continuously in a variety of camera shops and photo processing labs and as a freelance photographer. For her, a memorable moment in junior high turned into a life-long interest and career.

For many years, my wife and I worked in different school districts. One year, I decided to do something different and special for Valentine's Day by hiring a professional, all-female quartet to drop in unannounced and perform an impromptu concert in her classroom.

Naturally, my wife appreciated the gesture and enjoyed the surprise serenade. But it was even a bigger hit with her students.

Many had never witnessed any romantic act or expression between adults before. (Some of today's kids need to see proof that loving relationships are still possible.) For these students, this unexpected event was one they will never forget.

What started out to be a memorable moment for my wife ended up being an even more special moment for many of her students.

Naturally, school can't be all fun and games and special moments (like those above). We all know that a good education requires rigorous hard work and repeated drill and practice; but, often, it is the singular, stand-alone, and unexpected event that makes the most lasting impression.

Look around you at the schools and classrooms that are most popular and successful. What do they do differently? They probably pay attention to the wisdom of the welfare mom, make fun the way they do business, and work hard at creating magic moments for all kids. It's something any school can do, and it's not as hard as you think.

To prove the point, following is a starter kit of suggestions for giving students out-of-the-ordinary experiences and memorable moments that make school exciting and fun for young people:

- Be on TV.
- Get published.
- Visit backstage.
- Eat an oyster.
- Meet an author.
- Take a limo ride.
- Watch an animal giving birth.
- Go sailing.
- Make maple syrup.
- Observe a trial.
- Milk a cow.
- Attend a concert.
- Build a model house in the classroom. (I once knew a teacher who organized his entire semester's curriculum around having students construct a house big enough for them to walk around in. I'm sure

some of his students may have forgotten the teacher's name, but I bet none ever forgot "the house.")

- Ride along with a cop.
- Meet a sports hero up close and personal.
- Ride in a hot air balloon.
- Run the bases at a major league ball park.
- Play along with a professional band or orchestra.
- Make ice cream by hand.
- Attend a professional sports event. (In Minneapolis, a local benefactor annually provides tickets and transportation so kids from low-income families can attend a Timberwolves basketball game. For some, it is a once-in-a-lifetime experience.)
- Observe a surgeon performing surgery.
- Help out at a homeless shelter.
- Ride in a Hummer.
- Go out to breakfast with the teacher and order anything on the menu.
- Hold a baby.
- Attend a wedding. (It's extra special if it's their teacher's wedding.)
- Shake hands with a national political candidate.
- See snow or the ocean for the first time.

Obviously, none of the experiences above are costly or complicated. They don't have to be. They just have to spice up the humdrum routine of daily learning.

But why go to all the trouble? Or as one of my favorite teachers used to say, "What have we learned today?" Simply, that the welfare mom was right. Sometimes children really do need candy more than milk.

This is a lesson all school leaders need to hang on to. It needs to be passed on to each new generation of teachers. And in your school, unless you're lucky enough to have Mary Poppins on your staff, you get to do the passing.

Of all the things that matter most in running a school, this may not be the most important—unless, of course, you're a child. Then it may make all the difference.

17 A Chicken Doesn't Stop Scratching Just Because Worms Are Scarce

Things go bad. They get better. Every job has its little problems. That's why they call them "jobs," not "summer camp."

Harvey MacKay, CEO, author

Money problems are really idea problems.

Dr. Robert Scholler, nationally known minister

Lack of money is the root of all evil.

George Bernard Shaw, playwright

A problem is a chance to do your best.

Duke Ellington, musician

The folksy maxim in the title of this section is my favorite reminder that perseverance (second effort) is the antidote for adversity. It's similar to other popular truisms we've all grown up with and grown fond of (or sick of, as the case may be) such as

- If life hands you a lemon, make lemonade
- When the going gets tough, the tough get going
- Tough times don't last . . . tough people do

Don't roll your eyes. I know they're clichés. But clichés get a bum rap. Common axioms get overused and become clichés for a reason—because they ring true, strike a chord, and have universal applications. That's a lot to get out of a one-liner. Just because a principle or rule becomes a cliché, doesn't mean it's not valid.

This just might be a good time (maybe anytime is a good time) for school administrators to revisit the time-honored cliché. After all, for most school people, the worms are getting scarce.

Expectations and requirements are escalating, while resources are diminishing. Many schools have budget problems today. A great number have experienced severe budget cuts, including teacher layoffs. It's a difficult economic time to be a teacher—or a principal—or a superintendent.

Unfortunately, some administrators forget the lessons of the clichés. Instead of trying harder when money problems arise, they settle for whimpering and crying foul. That's not leadership; it's capitulation.

But like it or not, to some legislators, business leaders, taxpayers, and other non-parent public members, educators have become notorious for whining and bellyaching.

In addition to the 3-R's, too many school officials are now known for the 3-W's:

1. Why me?

2. Woe is me.

3. Weep for me!

This is not a winning image.

Even though edu-leaders have lots of legitimate gripes, chronic whining doesn't help. Crepe-hangers and crybabies don't make good leaders, and complaining never solves problems.

When the controversial ex-wrestler Jessie Ventura was governor of Minnesota, he often referred to education as a "black hole." According to Ventura, no matter how much money is thrown into public education, it's never enough. It all gets swallowed up.

Of course, it was overstated; but Jessie had a point. I've known some teacher unions that would never be satisfied. And some school boards, superintendents, and principals who would complain that any size budget isn't enough. It's complainers like that who give all of us a bad name and convince others that Ventura's black hole theory just might be true after all.

I recently heard of a company called Despair, Inc., that uses gallows humor to capitalize on society's growing disillusionment and cynicism. The company sells products such as half-empty mugs, frowny face icons, and lithographs with grim messages (e.g., "It is always darkest before—it gets pitch black"). It's warped, but it sells. I know some school administrators who must own stock in this outfit.

When school officials complain too often or too much, the very people they want to impress get tired of hearing it. It's like the old story of the shepherd boy and his constant wolf alerts. After a while, people stop listening. Too much complaining only makes matters worse.

In tough economic times, some principals and superintendents sulk, wring their hands, and gnash their teeth. Others pick up the pieces and press fiercely forward. Guess who the real leaders are. Adversity calls for more leadership, not more whining.

Instead of playing "poor me" or inviting people to a pity party, the key to resolving or outlasting bad situations is to "keep on keeping on" (keep scratching) and exert extra effort where necessary. There is always one more thing to try ("As long as one keeps searching, the answers come." —Joan Baez, musician). It must be those darn clichés at work all over again.

School administrators don't get to be real leaders by handling smooth sailing. They get there by overcoming adversity. Problems and crises (including budget woes) are really rites of passage for leaders.

Handling setbacks requires the ability to hunker down, remain confident, maintain perspective, see opportunities, weigh options, make decisions, react quickly—and, most of all, to try harder. Dealing with economic and other reversals is a test. If you pass, you're well on your way to becoming a successful leader.

There are many examples of school administrators who are eager and willing to lead the charge when the coffers are full, but who back off, back up, and back down when money is hard to come by.

Fortunately, there are even more examples of leaders who face economic downturns with second effort and follow the Irish writer Samuel Beckett's admonition: "Ever tried? Ever failed? No matter. Try again. Fail again. Fail better."

Following is a typical illustration of increased effort during hard times:

During the 1970s, a leading suburban school district near Minneapolis experienced an unexpected economic free fall.

The district was the first in the area to suffer a sudden sharp enrollment decline. (Other districts suffered similar downturns later.)

Within a relatively short period, the number of students plummeted from over 11,000 to a little more than 4,000.

In rapid succession, five of eleven schools had to be closed, horrendous staff layoffs occurred (reaching even tenured teachers with decades of experience and seniority in the district), and the budget was slashed by millions of dollars. It was any superintendent's worse nightmare.

If there was ever a time for moaning and groaning, this was it. And a lot of that went on. But another sound, even louder, soon could be heard in the background: the sound of scratching—the noise of school leaders and staff members who redoubled their efforts to find solutions and maintain a quality program.

The belabored district didn't fold, dissolve, merge, declare bankruptcy, or become a ward of the state. Instead, district administrators found a way to sell some empty schools, rent out other unused properties, and convert still others to self-supporting (or profit-making) community centers.

The school system reinvented itself as a resource for lifelong learning, serving all residents from the "womb to the tomb" and creating an award-winning Community Education program.

Additionally, despite the fact that 87% of the population had no children of traditional school age, the community was convinced to pass a series of excess levy referendums that brought in more discretionary local dollars than that enjoyed by any other system in the state.

As a result, the system resurfaced as a vibrant "lighthouse" district again. Later, every school (elementary and secondary) in the district was named a National School of Excellence by the federal government, the high school was designated one of the top 500 in the country, and the district's Spanish Immersion School was identified as one of the four best schools in the state. The system remains successful today.

All parties involved agreed that the school district's turnaround wasn't an accident, a fluke, or a miracle. But it was a testimony to what working more and wailing less can accomplish.

Of course, examples are all well and good, but they don't really reveal how a well-intentioned school leader can keep "scratching" when money is scarce (e.g., what do you do and how do you do it?). So here are some of the best ideas I know of (if you know better ones, tell the rest of us):

- Radiate confidence. Adopt a "We're going to get through this" attitude.
- Model a fiscal fitness mindset. Make efficiency and cost-effectiveness the normal way you do business every day.
- Tell your story without whining. Tell the truth. Don't exaggerate. ("Truth creates money, lies destroy it." —Suze Orman, financial guru and author)

- Remain true to your principles. Try to cut costs without cutting essential programs.
- Don't rush to raise taxes. Build a solid case first. Remember that the word *tax* comes from the Latin derivative meaning "to touch sharply." If you touch too quickly, too often, or too sharply, you may alienate the very supporters you need most.
- Emphasize all the things all great schools do that don't cost anything (e.g., set high expectations, keep focused on individual pupils, involve parents, and build a history of excellence).
- Maximize existing sources of revenue, including previously established taxing authority, fines, fees, grants, and gifts.
- Try to do more with less by enforcing economies, simplifying the bureaucracy, using more volunteers, outsourcing, and working smarter.
- Divest peripheral responsibilities. Get the community to take back some of the load.
- Become a "Prospector." Find, raise, and attract new money by being visible, going where the money is, and having a wish list.
- Try some creative fund-raising. For example, the fresh ideas below have worked for some of your peers—

    Sponsor a bowl-a-thon

    Hold a dog wash

    Initiate a "Migrating Flamingo" game. Place pink flamingos in people's yards and charge to have them removed or sent to someone else. (You can raise even more money by selling "insurance" for keeping flamingos away.)

    Let contributors determine what color to dye the principal's hair by putting donations in different colored jars. The jar containing the most money at the end is the chosen new hair color.

- Optimize the revenue-producing potential of school facilities and equipment. Consider renting out gyms, weight rooms, pools, stadiums, shops, practice rooms, darkrooms, computer labs, phone banks, and food service facilities.
- Start a School Foundation offering a full range of charitable-giving options and access to gift-planning assistance to help provide enhanced financial support for your schools.

Naturally, none of these strategies alone will solve your school's serious funding problems. But they will demonstrate to all those who depend on you that they are not powerless, that they still have options, and that, as leader, you are willing to work harder to make good things happen. Sometimes during periods of retrenchment, what you do is not as important as the fact that you are doing something.

The bottom line is that perseverance ranks right up there with passion in determining school leader success. The old cliché about continuing to scratch even when worms are scarce is as valid today as it ever was.

If you don't know it already, don't let this timeless lesson get by you: THE BEST RESPONSE TO ADVERSITY IS RENEWED EFFORT! Read it again. Repeat it. Take it to heart.

In tough times, effective school leaders don't quit or merely settle for cursing their fate. They work harder. Why? The most eloquent answer I've heard comes from Shiran Ebad, the first Muslim woman to win the Nobel Peace Prize (2003). When asked why she kept working for human rights against overwhelming odds, Ebad simply replied, "The duty of life is to fight in a difficult situation."

I can't improve on that. Just believe it. Act on it. It's what real leaders do. And that's no cliché.

18 The Reverse Side Has a Reverse Side

So many men, so many opinions.

Terence, Roman poet

Men are not agreed on any one thing.

Montaigne, 16th century essayist

We are of different opinions at different hours but we always may be said to be at heart on the side of truth.

Ralph Waldo Emerson, American philosopher–writer

American public education is short of many things, but opinion isn't one of them. Every issue affecting your school has, at least, two sides—often more. (That's why they call them issues, not givens.)

Every aspect of schools and schooling seems to provoke multiple responses and viewpoints. As the Japanese say, "The reverse side also has a reverse side." That's why every position you take as a school administrator has an opposing view. Get used to it.

Differences of opinion just come naturally to people who care for or about kids. Things always look differently depending on where you're from, where you're standing, or where you're going. When Lady Godiva took her famous ride, people on opposite sides of the street had entirely different views. It may not always be that dramatic, but the same thing happens in your schools every day.

Anyone who hangs around this business long enough and pays attention learns that education lends itself to varied interpretations and that more than one opinion can be a legitimate viewpoint.

Most issues in public education are not black and white. At best they are two shades of dingy gray. Few positions are all right or all wrong or mutually exclusive. Everyone owns a piece of the truth. If you want to excel as a principal or superintendent, you need to learn to see what's right about others' opinions. Empathy is a cornerstone of successful leadership.

Being a school leader isn't about winning all the time. It's not necessary that your ideas always prevail, but that the best ideas always prevail.

If you insist on always winning, you jeopardize your credibility. Every time you "win," you make a potential enemy. If you insist on always winning, you may end up with nothing but enemies. It's always lonely at the top, but it shouldn't be that lonely.

Nevertheless, some principals and superintendents have to be "right" all the time—even if they have to use "whips and chains" to convince others. It's a career-ending strategy.

"My way or the highway" is no way to run a school. Sometimes, victory at all costs costs too much, and winning can become a losing proposition.

A school leader's job—your job—is to get things done. You can't do that through one-way warfare or continuous standoffs. You do it by understanding where others are coming from and why, appreciating that others can have valid views and honest emotions too, and figuring out how to reconcile differences. It's called compromise.

Sometimes compromising gets a bad rap for lacking principle, courage, or conviction. This may be true in a military organization, but not in a public institution. (And nothing is more public than the public schools.)

Compromise is the tool of choice for creative leaders in the public sector. Without it, few bills would ever become law, few levy referendums would succeed, and few labor contracts would ever get settled. In fact, without compromise, there would be no U.S. Constitution, no America as we know it, and no viable system of public education in this country.

For successful school leaders, giving up a little to gain a lot is not a sigh of wishy-washy weakness. It's tough-minded pragmatism. In education, leadership is often a matter of trade-offs.

Look at the decisions you've made recently. How many involved or resulted from compromises? If most of them were unilateral, you may be performing like a one-man band instead of like the conductor of an orchestra.

Look over your shoulder. If no one is following, you may no longer be in charge. That's what happens when administrators become intractable or refuse to yield, bend, or bargain.

We hear a lot these days about *cooperative learning* that minimizes competition and avoids creating winners and losers. Maybe we should be hearing more about "cooperative leading" as well.

Lasting leaders are not afraid to compromise. They accept the simultaneous existence of opposites and see the truth on both sides. (There is always plenty of truth to go around.)

If you are doing your job right, your days are full of compromises, great and small—each moving you closer to your goals. Effective school leaders don't compromise basic education goals, moral and ethical values, or the safety and welfare of children. But everything else is negotiable.

Compromise is simply the art of doing all that is possible at the time. Isn't that what you were hired to do?

The nation's most successful principals and superintendents are always self-confident enough to give and take a little. Horse-trading is a leadership tool that never goes out of style when you want to achieve maximum results.

There's another good reason for remaining open to compromise. You just might be wrong, and those with a different opinion might turn out to be right. Benjamin Franklin made the point clear in his eloquent closing remarks at the Constitutional Convention:

> For, having lived long, I have experienced many instances of being obliged, by better information or further consideration, to change opinions, even on important subjects, which I once thought right, but found to be otherwise.

On those occasions when you actually do change your mind, you will be glad you compromised. If compromise was good enough for Franklin and the other Founding Fathers, it's probably good enough for you and me.

As chief executive of the school, every time you turn around, you are confronted with divergent opinions—some mundane, some monumental—that afford opportunities for conflict or compromise. Choose compromise whenever possible.

You don't need total victory or unconditional surrender on every issue. You just need to see some small, incremental progress. Sometimes, like baseball, school leadership is a game of inches.

Fortunately, in many school situations, the schism between varying viewpoints isn't as great as it seems. For instance, church and state are separated; but they are not entirely divorced. There is still plenty of room for personal faith and prayer in the public schools. I don't know any good administrator who survives without them.

Compromise is so common in a school leader's life that you may not be fully aware of it. Following are examples of true-to-life compromise situations—the kind that occur in your school every day.

- **Issue:** The school board wants to build a large high school capable of accommodating several thousand students. Administrators think smaller is better.
  Compromise: Build a large high school designed around a "house plan" of organization (e.g., schools-within-a-school)

- **Issue:** Science teachers insist on teaching the theory of evolution. Many influential parents and some school board members demand that students learn about creationism.
  Compromise: Teach both.

- **Issue:** Parents and administrators want evening parent conferences to accommodate families in which both parents work. Teachers don't want to work any more hours.
  Compromise: Grant teachers *comp time*: Trade off evening conference time for an equivalent amount of released time (e.g., the day after Thanksgiving).

- **Issue:** Some middle school parents believe their children learn best in a flexible environment. Other parents favor a more traditional structure.
  Compromise: Form two middle schools (one with a modular, flexible schedule and one with a conventional format) and allow parents a choice (open enrollment) between the two.

- **Issue:** The school board is split over two final high school principal candidates.
  Compromise: Select one candidate as principal and the other as associate principal.

- **Issue:** Parents are adamant that more students are qualified for the school's cheerleading squad than are actually selected. The cheerleading advisor is equally adamant that squad size must be limited to be manageable.
  Compromise: Establish multiple cheerleading squads for different sports or seasons.

- **Issue:** The administration must cut down on the number of course offerings to contain costs. Parents and students want to retain all existing courses.
  Compromise: Offer affected courses on alternate years.

- **Issue:** The school board undertakes a multischool construction program. Some board members favor bringing in a nationally known architect to design the project. Other members believe a local architect should be selected.

    Compromise: Split the project between the outside architect and a local firm.

- **Issue:** The teaching staff is divided between the American Federation of Teachers (AFT) and the National Education Association (NEA) as their choice for exclusive bargaining representative.

    Compromise: Merge the two unions into one unit. (It works in Minnesota where the consolidated bargaining agent is called simply "Education Minnesota.")

- **Issue:** Clerical unit members feel underpaid. Custodial union members think no bargaining unit should receive greater salary increases than another.

    Compromise: Adopt a single salary schedule covering both units based on the concept of "comparable worth."

- **Issue:** Parents of a severely disabled child want their student mainstreamed. The faculty doesn't feel equipped or ready to accommodate such an extreme handicapped condition in the regular classroom.

    Compromise: Initiate a limited trial schedule (e.g., two hours a day) for the pupil and evaluate the results.

Sound familiar? Obviously, differences of opinion make up much of the daily life within the school. Without compromise, it's easy to get bogged down in bickering and babbling. As long as there are opposing voices, someone has to try to get them all speaking from the same text. The school leader comes to mind. If you don't do it, who will?

Of course, some issues defy compromise. When there is absolutely no middle ground for agreement, the only recourse is to pick a side and agree to disagree. But wise leaders always seek compromise first and take unilateral or arbitrary action only as a last resort. Even then, it always pays to leave the door ajar for possible future efforts and overtures to reconcile the opposing positions.

Benjamin Franklin again likened the process of political compromise to the winning strategies in the game of chess (e.g., never rush an opponent, be willing occasionally to lose a point to gain a friend, and never gloat over a perceived victory). It's not a bad metaphor, but it needs fleshing out.

What works best in reconciling differing factions is to follow the tactics used by expert negotiators:

1. Avoid an either or mentality as much as possible.

2. Communicate as clearly and honestly as you can, and listen as carefully as you are capable of. ("When men understand what each other mean, they see, for the most part, that controversy is either superfluous or hopeless." —Cardinal Newman, British theologian.)

3. Don't wage war over trifles. Follow popular author Richard Carlson's advice: "Don't sweat the small stuff." Save your "sound and fury" for issues that matter most.

4. Be respectful no matter how contentious differences become.

5. Keep personalities and individual character out of the debate.

6. Use humor to dissipate tension and hostility. Look for the ridiculous and the silliness in the dispute. It's always there. Be willing to laugh at yourself and with others. Laughter trumps anger in most situations.

7. Find the common ground, no matter how minute or inconsequential it may seem. There is almost always something the parties can agree upon.

8. Tackle the easiest facets of the dispute first. Build on small agreements.

9. Be satisfied with small gains. Rome wasn't built in a—well, you know the rest. ("Half a loaf is still bread." —Robert Half, pioneer in the temporary help industry.)

10. Remain gracious throughout the process, regardless of what position ultimately prevails.

11. Contend in private and show solidarity in public. There is a reason that, following every summit meeting, heads of state are always photographed together to demonstrate apparent amiability, despite private differences. When disputes go public, compromise becomes much more difficult.

12. Don't quit. Keep striving for greater agreement. Effective leaders always leave doors open (or at least unlocked) and never burn bridges completely.

Democracy means dissent. That's why leaders in every organization— perhaps in the public schools even more than most—deal with differences and face off with opposing factions on a regular basis. That's part of the job. That's why the job exists.

So who makes the best school leader: a combatant who must always win, or a healer who seeks compromise so everyone wins? You be the judge.

Here, then, is the take-home lesson from this section: In public education there can be many views, but only one vision. As a principal or superintendent, it is your responsibility to blend the views and tend to the vision.

"The reverse side also has a reverse side" is not only a Japanese proverb; it is an everlasting principle in school leadership. If you or anyone else disagrees— I rest my case.

19 The Best Leader Is a "Servant Leader"

Service is not optional.

Rick Warren, inspirational author

The only really happy people are those who have learned to serve.

Albert Schweitzer, Nobel Peace Prize
winning philosopher, physician, and missionary

The term *servant leader* is a popular buzz phrase among school administrators today. In fact, leaders in all fields are buzzing about it. But what does it mean?

It sounds like an oxymoron. How can a principal or superintendent be a servant? And why would any administrator want to be?

When I was a kid in school, principals didn't act like servants. They weren't expected to be servants. In those days, it was the school leader's job to "control" the school, the students, and the teachers. They led by administrative fiat. They gave orders and made rules—and enforced them.

Most of the administrators I remember managed by fear and motivated by invective, intimidation, and coercion. The principal was the "boss." Teachers and pupils were expected to follow rules and obey directives without discussion or dissent.

Back then, no one had ever heard of empowerment, shared decision making, or site-based management. Hierarchal status was all-important and decisions were always handed down from the top. School leaders seemed more interested in "serve us" than in service.

Of course, there were occasions when it was advantageous for administrators to create the appearance or perception of serving the needs or wishes of students and staff members, in order to look good themselves. Unfortunately, these occurrences of "cosmetic service" were usually short-lived.

What was more common was for administrators to distance themselves from others in order to maintain a certain mystique. Familiarity was viewed as a sign of weakness.

Surprisingly, this rigid form of military leadership seemed to work in schools at the time. I'm certain, however, that the principals and superintendents I knew as a youth wouldn't make it in today's schools.

What's changed? Everything: Students. Teachers. Families. Society. Expectations. Politics. Financing. Technology. It's difficult to think of any aspect of schooling that hasn't been altered dramatically since I was a student.

That's why successful school leaders have evolved from practicing macho management years ago to employing maestro management today. What happened to upend the old paradigm?

For starters, there is no such thing as inherent positional authority in today's schools. Principals and superintendents don't receive respect just because they have an administrative title. They have to earn it.

In return, teachers and other staff members want respect for themselves today. They want some autonomy and a piece of the action. They want (and often demand) to be listened to and to be kept in the loop about what's going on in the organization (good and bad) and what's coming down the road (e.g., budget cuts, salary freezes, layoffs, building closings, crowded classrooms, etc.). Most of all, they want opportunities for growth and a share in decision making.

Today's young teachers don't want any more rules. They want some slack. They simply want to be respected for what they do, supported and recognized for good performance, respected as individuals, and treated as adults.

Whoa! That's a big order. Obviously, the old paradigm of school administration doesn't fit any longer. Of course, there still are some old-style school managers left. (Dinosaurs die slowly.) I can name a few, but they are rapidly becoming extinct.

More and more principals and superintendents now are switching from rule making and bossing people around to collaborating and orchestrating. They are looking for ways to give school personnel whatever they need to get the job done. Increasingly, effective school leaders are serving the needs of those they lead. But how do they do it? If principals and superintendents can't control and order others around anymore, what can you do?

How about pointing your staff members in the right direction, setting them up for success, and getting out of the way? How about identifying what teachers need to succeed first, and then working backwards to determine how you can help them? How about motivating staff members and, then, running interference for them?

If you are not leading your school the way these questions suggest, you may have some catching up to do. This is the new paradigm.

Serving the needs of teachers so they can better serve the needs of students, the community, and the organization is the new direction of school leadership. Whoever advised, "Take care of your employees so they can take care of business," could become the spokesperson for today's school leaders.

In *Living a Life That Matters,* Harold S. Kushner suggests that great leaders shouldn't aspire to winning an award for best actor in the organization, but rather should strive to be the *best supporting actor* in the organization.

This may sound like a radical new concept, but it's not. Servant leadership was even mentioned in the Bible (Mark 10:3). Jesus was the greatest example.

If you want to succeed and excel as leader of a great school these days, you may not have to wash the feet of your followers, but you will have to support them, nurture them, protect them, serve them—and lead by influence, rather than by edict.

It all starts with an attitude. Servant leadership is mostly a mind-set. As principal or superintendent you are only as good as the teachers and other staff members who work for you. And they are only as good as you allow and equip them to be. To run a successful modern school, you have to believe this, act on it, and let it show in your attitude. But how?

Of course, there are countless ways to demonstrate an attitude of service leadership in your school. Below are ten of the best. (They're not new, but they are guaranteed to make you a better leader and your school a better place to work and learn.)

1. Get to know every employee as a unique human being. Know them by more than their names. Learn something about their families, their lives outside of school, their interests, and what makes them tick. Try listening more than you speak. You don't have to become a close friend of everyone on your staff. They already have friends. But you should be friendly, accessible, caring, sensitive, and supportive. You can't serve teachers unless you know who they are and what they really need.

2. Become a world-class "noticer." Notice what's going on, what's working, where the hitches, hang-ups, and logjams are, and what needs to be done to make teachers, clerks, custodians, and other employees more productive.

3. Practice "open management." Keep staff members fully informed about *all* matters that affect them. Tell the truth, the whole truth, and nothing but—you know the drill.

4. Model productive behavior. Lead by influence.

5. Make empowerment more than a catchy management cliché. Don't just delegate responsibilities. Delegate authority and resources as well.

6. Buffer school employees from distracting intrusions and interruptions.

7. Trade in micromanaging for teaching, mentoring, coaching, and cheerleading.

8. Give students and staff members lots of choices and second chances.

9. Find a way to offer needed training and growth opportunities to all staff members, not just teachers.

10. Prospect for resources. Do whatever it takes to get what your staff needs to meet their goals (e.g., more budget, time, tools, space, and materials).

If you've been paying close attention, you may have noticed that much of what a servant leader does doesn't cost a thing. What many teachers need most to achieve peak performance is just your time, attention, recognition, trust, a helping hand, a pat on the back, or a shoulder to cry on. They're all free.

What you may not have noticed is that creating conditions where staff members can do their best work may also mean helping out in their personal lives (e.g., recommending a counselor, arranging a credit union loan, or finding temporary housing, etc.).

Work and home life can get blurred. We all bring work home occasionally. Likewise, some of us sometimes bring our home life to work, and the work suffers.

There are times when being a true servant leader requires being helpful and supportive off the job as well as on the job.

My wife learned this lesson early on, even before we were married, while she was still in her first year of teaching. In their rush to get ready for their first teaching jobs, she and her two roommates made a very poor choice of landlords.

After only a few weeks into the school year, their landlord began exhibiting some bizarre behavior. He started making a number of strange and outrageous accusations. Among other things, he falsely claimed that the young women held wild, drunken parties. He even went so far as to search the trash in hopes of getting fingerprints as evidence from discarded wine bottles. He also accused them of "slamming down the toilet seat in an unlady-like manner" and bringing in bugs that inhabited and damaged his lampshades. Naturally, the roommates grew increasingly uneasy and uncomfortable with their living arrangements.

The final straw came when they discovered signs that he had entered their apartment and snooped around while they were at school. For three single young women, this was scary.

A hurried decision was made to bring in one of the roommate's parents to secure the apartment during the school day and to move out as soon as possible. Naturally, the three roommates felt pressured, stressed, and distracted at home and at work. They had to find a new place to live and someplace to store their furniture until they could move in, while dealing with the overwhelming demands and deadlines of a brand new job at the same time.

What worried them the most was that school officials might believe the landlord's accusations and begin to question their stability.

Their anxiety peaked later when their ex-landlord ran a want ad announcing, "Attractive two-bedroom apartment for rent. Good location. No first-year teachers allowed." Once the ad appeared, the roommates were more worried than ever that the district might regret hiring them.

Of course, it all worked out—with a little help from some sensitive school administrators. First, my future wife's principal came to the rescue immediately by offering to store their furniture on the school's stage. Later, the assistant superintendent personally assured the three beginners that the district administration stood by them, gave no credence to the landlord's allegations, continued to have full confidence in them, and was there to help if needed. Whew! (R-O-L-A-I-D-S isn't the only way to spell relief.)

The school leaders could easily have compounded the problem by criticizing or expressing doubt or, worse yet, by doing nothing and leaving the new teachers wondering where they stood. Instead, they gave their new staff members what they needed most—loyalty and support. That's all it took to free up three beginners to do their best.

The whole unpleasant and embarrassing situation could have cast a shadow over the young women's initial year of teaching and, perhaps, derailed three promising careers. As it turned out, all three had a good first year and went on to have successful careers in the district.

It wasn't a big deal to anyone, except to three fledgling teachers. It would have been no surprise if administrators had ignored or sloughed off the whole incident. They didn't need to get involved. It wasn't really a school matter. But it mattered to the three beginners. That's why these school leaders made a point to demonstrate overt support.

Their expression of support was the kind of small, everyday act that characterizes school leaders committed to helping staff members. Nobody ever said servant leadership had to be glamorous or dramatic.

You see (and hopefully perform) acts of servant leadership all the time. Some are monumental. Some are menial. All are important.

Here are more examples of the kinds of things (great and small) that good administrators do to serve staff members so they can better serve kids:

- Find space for one-on-one help for disabled students.
- Loan out laptops for teachers to work with at home.
- Limit the number of new programs at any one time.
- Require groups that rent school space to clean up so regular custodians don't have to.
- Spread out problem kids.
- Get the parent organization to conduct all fund-raising activities (candy sales, magazine drives, etc.) outside of regular class time.
- Install phones in all classrooms.
- Allow released time for curriculum committee work.
- Solicit donations of previously owned musical instruments to help beef up band and orchestra programs and allow more kids to participate.
- Keep the media out of the classroom.
- Buffer teachers from unreasonable parents or overzealous vendors.
- Give grade levels or subject area departments some discretionary funds.
- Bring in volunteers to "ride shotgun" on school buses so drivers can concentrate on safe driving rather than on crowd control.
- Come up with a little seed money for the teachers' pet projects.
- Allow teachers (and other staff members) to plan their own on-site, in-service, staff development programs.
- Give teachers compensatory time off for evening conferences and other required night activities.
- Recruit volunteer lay readers to help language arts teachers evaluate student writing.
- Reduce the number of classroom interruptions, including intercom announcements.
- Allow teachers to visit other schools to observe new programs and techniques.
- Grant salary lane-change credit for work on local curriculum or policy committees.
- Initiate interventions for staff members suffering from chemical dependency problems.
- Defend worthwhile programs that come under attack so teachers can spend their time teaching rather than defending their teaching.

These may be more examples than you want or need. The point is that opportunities for proving yourself a servant leader are unlimited.

We all know there are many ways to define leadership. But if you've read this far, you've probably picked up that my favorite is simply "removing obstacles." It's a different way to look at school administration.

Unfortunately, some principals and superintendents don't remove obstacles or roadblocks. They are the obstacles.

There is a better way. The wisest and best school leaders today are servant leaders. Rick Warren, author of *The Purpose Driven Life,* may say it best: "Service is the pathway to significance." It's a pathway more and more successful principals and superintendents are following. If you are not on the path yet, don't wait too long.

20 Your Mother Didn't Raise You to Be a Bureaucrat

Bureaucracy is the death of any achievement.

Albert Einstein, legendary physicist,
mathematician, and author of the "theory of relativity"

I learned from the army it's easier to tell the people in the office what they want to hear because if you don't there's always someone higher up who wants you to fill out a longer form.

Frank McCourt, prize-winning Irish author

Bureaucracy is the cancer of successful organizations—including schools. Every school leader should be required to take a vow—a blood oath—to stamp it out at every turn.

Most dictionaries define *bureaucracy* as "management marked by adherence to inflexible rules of operation and an inclination to follow complex procedures that impede effective action." Obviously, this is nasty stuff. You don't want it in your school.

Unfortunately, bureaucracy is subtle, insidious, and seductive. Members of Alcoholics Anonymous often describe alcohol as "cunning, baffling, and powerful." They could just as well be talking about bureaucracy.

Worse yet, bureaucracy is creepy. It can creep unnoticed into every facet of the organization until there is nothing else left but the hierarchies, the rules, the game playing, and the self-serving protocols.

● 145

Bureaucracy sucks. It can suck the life out of an organization and turn aspiring leaders into errand running, rule-bound, play-it-safe, rubber-stamping, paper-shuffling functionaries. It's not a pretty picture.

We've all seen talented teachers become promising principals only to end up clueless and soulless, doing more and more of the business of perpetuating the bureaucracy and less and less of the business of helping kids.

If you are reading this book, you obviously don't want this to be your career path. Your mother didn't raise you to be a bureaucrat. Of course, it doesn't have to happen. But how do you know if you are being sucked in?

It's not so terribly difficult. The warning signs are always there if you look closely. Try using the following informal instrument to help gauge your bureaucracy quotient:

As a school administrator, you may be a bureaucrat if—

- You spend more time with paper than with people.
- Someone else controls your calendar.
- You don't talk directly to individual students (or to individual teachers) as much as you used to.
- Outsiders have difficulty calling your office or school and actually talking to a human being.
- You keep adding more levels of approval.
- Your school has an official form to fill out for almost everything.
- You go to so many meetings that they all begin to blur together and you can't clearly remember one from another.
- Rules keep piling up. Your policy manual is now thicker than your curriculum guide.
- You have lots of employees with the word "assistant" in their title.
- You rely more and more on e-mail and voice mail and less and less on personal, face-to-face contact.
- People can't reach you without an appointment.
- You receive many written reports that you (or no one else) ever reads.
- The cost of administration is increasing disproportionately to growth of the overall budget.
- Turf battles are common in your school.
- You feel tired more often than you feel excited.
- You have a "committee on committees."
- The people around you tend to tell you only what they know you want to hear.
- You hear phrases like, "It's not my job," or "There's no reason; it's just policy" a lot.
- You are more comfortable with school board members and politicians than with teachers and kids.

- You are making more and more important decisions based on polls, surveys, and focus groups.
- The people who answer your school phones usually can't answer the questions or solve callers' problems. ("A sure sign of bureaucracy is when the first person who answers the phone can't help you." —"Wit of Wisdom," *Supervision Magazine*)
- Titles and status symbols are more important than they used to be.
- You think a lot about retirement and your pension.
- People have given up trying to implement change because there are too many hurdles to clear.
- You worry more about satisfying the media or keeping the school board happy than about helping kids.
- You have begun to accept image over substance.
- You spend a lot of energy on spin doctoring and CYA (Covering your—well, you know).
- People don't bring you problems or bad news anymore.
- You never have time to reflect or dream.
- You haven't changed anything (including your mind) in the last six months.
- You don't care as much as you used to.
- No one in the organization is having fun any more.

Well, how did you do? If the signs and symptoms aren't there, you're good for today. But you had better check again tomorrow.

Because it's easy to slip into routine, start going through the motions, stop taking risks, and settle for the status quo. It's comfortable. It's safe. It's acceptable. And it can happen quickly.

Bureaucracy is like a disease that spreads and grows silently and exponentially and eventually consumes all the available energy. Vigilance is the only known cure.

Strangely enough, it's not just newcomers and neophytes who must be wary. Veteran administrators are vulnerable too. Sometimes, the longer you are in a position—especially a position at the top—the easier it is to succumb to bureaucratic comfort.

Likewise, there are some jobs that are intentionally and inherently bureaucratic in nature. I've had a few. You have some in your system now. You may even be *in* one as we speak.

The real truth, however, is that no matter where you are or how long you've been there, you can bust out of the bureaucracy, reclaim clarity, and recapture your sense of purpose. But first, you have to want to.

I learned this lesson several years ago when I was placed in charge of the human resources department of a large suburban school district. The position was well established. Procedures were set. A calendar of prescribed activities was in place. The functions had become routinized. The job was mostly a matter of administering benefits and seeing that filing, processing, and record keeping occurred as scheduled.

Needless to say, the job wasn't much fun. And it wasn't fulfilling. It was downright boring. It was—well, uh—*bureaucratic!*

Doing this kind of work wasn't why I became an educator. The rest of the staff felt equally uninspired and unchallenged. So we decided to do something about it.

Over the next several months, we set about redefining our department as the "People Office," emphasizing service to all employees. Our goal was to reduce hassles, simplify life, and enhance the work of all staff members so that they could do a better job of helping kids.

We began by reorganizing the office space to be more accessible and user-friendly. We also distributed an employee handbook outlining how we could help people satisfy legal requirements, meet deadlines, simplify paperwork, capitalize on growth opportunities, boost income potential, and get the most from their contractual benefits.

Later, we followed up with a periodic newsletter containing more personnel tips and updates. Likewise, a conscious effort was made to open up communication and develop more positive relationships with all employee unions.

We also made special efforts to get staff members their favorite substitute teacher during necessary absences. At year's end, we introduced for the first time a recognition program to celebrate and honor all substitutes ("Guest Teachers") who worked in the district.

And finally, we inaugurated an exciting "Star Search" program to attract and hire the "best and brightest" graduating education students in the state.

What happened? Our efforts paid off. The ho-hum human resources department that people once saw as a necessary evil in the organization was reinvented as a friendly place to go for service and help.

People noticed the transformation. Morale throughout the organization actually improved as a result. And making the system as better place for adults to work made it a better place for kids to learn as well.

The "People Office" was a hit. Consequently, all of us involved felt we were doing something valuable to improve the school system. It felt good. Work was fun again.

Years later with different leadership the department eventually lapsed into its old routines, practices, procedures, and protocols. Once again, it became more of a watchdog than an advocate. Bureaucracy was resurrected.

But we had proved to ourselves that it didn't have to be that way. You can prove it in your own job or organization as well.

In fairness, a little bureaucracy may be a good thing to provide some structure and guard against chaos. But the more bureaucratic an organization becomes, the less likely it is to be creative or responsive. That's why bureaucracies can get by with mere managers, while creative organizations (like your school) need real leaders. There is a difference:

Bureaucratic managers	*Effective leaders*
Protect	Project
React	Proact
Control	Empower
Defend	Extend
Make rules	Set goals
Meet standards	Raise the bar
Stress policies	Stress possibilities
Refine the present	Define the future
Enforce rules to maintain status quo	Stretch, bend, and break rules to achieve new goals
Answer the same old questions	Ask new questions

Since you've stuck with this book this far, it's pretty obvious that you want to be a real leader for your school, not just manager of another bureaucratic training mill. This means you need to actively resist the temptation to settle for a perfunctory role.

The following strategies have helped other school leaders keep their head in the game, reduce obstructive rules or procedures, and focus on doing what matters most. They may do the same for you if you let them. Take a look and use what you like. You have nothing to lose but a membership in Bureaucrats Anonymous.

- Memorize the school's mission statement. Make it your mantra. Repeat it often. (Note it doesn't say anything about constructing and caring for a bureaucracy.)
- Maximize your direct contact with students. Schedule time in classrooms. Attend student events. Eat lunch with kids. In some high schools, administrators actually teach at least a one-semester class each year. Bill Edwards, principal of Washburn Rural High School (Kansas), has gone so far as to take an occasional role in the school's musical productions. Anything you can do to keep students foremost in your mind keeps bureaucracy on the back burner.

- Look for ways to flatten the school's hierarchy. Try to get along with fewer assistants. Make it a habit to look at the possibility of eliminating or consolidating positions before filling vacancies.
- Limit the number of meetings. Dr. Richard J. Soghoian, headmaster of Columbia Grammar and Prep School, refuses altogether to have conference rooms, meetings, or committees. He calls them "a recipe for yakking and procrastination." Soghoian may have a point. Try declaring a "Non-meeting Day" once in a while, and begin each meeting you do have with the question, "Why are we in business?"
- Wage war on paperwork. Solicit ideas for reducing red tape. Give a prize (e.g., a free lunch, gift certificate to a popular local coffee house, or movie tickets) for the best suggestion.
- Audit your policies to make sure they are supportive of kids, not just a convenience for adults.
- Take time to retrace the path of a new idea from inspiration to implementation. What hurdles had to be cleared? How long did it take? How much paperwork was involved? How many approvals were required? If the progression was overly complicated and cumbersome, start streamlining the way ideas become action. Alacrity is the mark of a winning organization.
- Make it a habit to put all new practices and procedures to the "What has this got to do with kids?" test.
- Decorate every office with pictures of children. It reminds staff members to stay focused on the main thing and not get distracted by made-up or phony work.
- Invite students to staff meetings. Include them on site counsels, advisory panels, and curriculum committees. A student presence keeps adults honest and on task.
- Hold contests to identify dumb rules, forms, or procedures.
- Assign people to tasks on the basis of talent, not titles.
- Borrow a page from your business counterparts and start relying more on cross-disciplinary teams than on separate and discreet departments.
- Network with the best leaders you know. A bureaucratic attitude is contagious. Limit your exposure.
- Conduct your own reality check. Have selected associates call your school office with a question or problem. See how they are treated, how much help they receive, and how quickly they get satisfaction. If you don't like the results, make necessary changes.

These simple steps can help hold bureaucracy at bay in your school. Naturally, you and your staff can think of many other safeguards and preventative measures. It's worth doing. Bureaucracy doesn't take over an organization by design, but by default. If it happens on your watch, "de fault" is yours.

The real problem with bureaucracy is that it confuses protecting and preserving the organizational structure with achieving its goals. The more bureaucratic a system becomes, the more difficult it is to keep the central purpose in mind.

It's a little like the popular children's holiday classic, *The Polar Express,* by Chris Van Allsburg. In the story, only small children can hear the crystalline clear sound of a bell taken from Santa's sleigh. As they grow older, the children gradually lose their ability to hear the bell distinctly. Grown-ups can no longer hear it at all.

In the real world, bureaucracy can cause you to cease to believe and rob you of the capacity to hear the bell inside that called you to become an educator in the first place.

If that happens, your mother is going to be deeply disappointed. Do not ask for whom the bell tolls. It tolls for you. Do you still hear it?

21 Politicians and Armchair Quarterbacks Don't Get It—So You Have To

You will always find some Eskimos willing to instruct the Congolese on how to cope with heat waves.

Unknown

If 50 million people say a foolish thing, it is still a foolish thing.

Anatole France, French critic, satirist,
and Nobel Prize for Literature recipient

Some critics are like chimney sweepers; they put out the fire below, and frighten the swallows above; They scrape a long time in the chimney, cover themselves with soot; and bring nothing away but a box of cinders, and they sing from the top of the house as if they had built it.

Henry Wadsworth Longfellow, American poet

Some well-intentioned citizens, as well as many critics and wannabe reformers (including lawmakers and other elected officials), think that "Education is too important to be left to the professionals."

Unfortunately, an important corollary that is often missing from the public conscience is, "Education is too important to be left to amateurs."

Naturally, the public schools are a public conversation piece (and rightly so.) It's what people talk about around the water cooler, in the carpool, after church, before the movie, at the Little League field, over cards, over coffee, and in the hallowed Halls of Legislatures. The scary thing is that most people don't know what they are talking about.

Congratulations—you have the distinction of being a leader in a field where everyone is a self-appointed expert and many outsiders think they know more about your domain than you do. How does that make you feel?

Apparently, if you want to know how to run a school, you don't have to take graduate courses or read books like this. You can just listen to all the Monday morning quarterbacks who speak with the authority of 20-20 hindsight. They all think they know what's wrong with the public schools—including your school—and how to fix it.

The problem is that most people who talk the most about public education (some of whom end up making policy and funding decisions affecting schools) speak from a built-in bias, inaccurate or incomplete information, or an imperfect understanding of what's involved. They just don't get it.

All that most people really "know" about today's public schools is derived from what they get from the media, from their own nostalgic memories of a school system that never was, from what their own kids tell them, or from talking to others just like themselves.

In addition, many of the voices expounding about the schools are driven by narrow interests. They tend to care about taxes or test scores or civil rights issues or football wins and losses or only what affects their own child at the moment—and not much more.

That's why many of those who cry out the loudest and longest about today's schools just don't get it—

- Politicians don't get it.
- The courts don't get it.
- Business leaders don't get it.
- Parents don't get it.
- Focus groups don't get it.
- The media doesn't get it.
- Sometimes, school boards and teacher unions don't get it.
- Even education professors and education writers (this author included) don't always get it.

Your life is full of examples of individuals and groups having a voice and taking a stand but missing the point. Following are ten firsthand cases in point:

1. I know a school board that takes great pride in having built an enormous and expensive high school on a beautiful campus that accommodates up to 3,000 pupils. Unfortunately, this board is a wake-up call away from reality. Education isn't a mob activity. Bigger isn't better. Kids don't need a Taj Mahal to learn best. What they require is simply good teachers who know them and what they need.

2. I know a governor who slashed funding for early childhood education and then proposed hiring a few $100,000 superteachers to help lift lagging inner-city schools. I'm afraid the governor doesn't get it.

3. I know several politicians who believe adding more tests constitutes educational reform. What are they thinking?

4. I know states that support zero-tolerance weapons policies and the creation of "safe-zones" around schools and then pass "conceal and carry" laws that allow people to carry guns onto school property as a matter of constitutional right. Huh?

5. I know successful business leaders who think today's kids are a hopelessly lost generation—except for their own children and grandchildren, of course.

6. I've known state auditors who raised a hue and cry about superintendents' salaries. And I've known newspapers that can't stop writing about the high cost of school administration. They all miss the point that school leaders make only a pittance compared to similar CEOs and ranking executives in most other enterprises. Since when did leadership become a cheap commodity?

7. I once knew a school board that actually ordered the school administration to see to it that all students are above average. (No, it wasn't Garrison Keillor's mythical Lake Woebegone.)

8. I know many parents (and legislators) who think school choice is a panacea. Wrong.

9. I know of a few minority leaders who vigorously (and successfully) opposed the selection of a new superintendent because he was not a minority and they had not been consulted—even though he had been handpicked by the popular outgoing superintendent (who was a minority) and possessed unequaled, impeccable credentials for

dealing with business and political leaders and other power brokers who held the future of the school district in their hands. It's too bad that this vocal minority missed the point that leadership doesn't always have to be about race or cosmetic selection processes, but should always be about picking the right person for the job at the right time.

10. I also know political leaders who think they're helping by mandating programs without funding them. And they do it repeatedly. It never works, but they never get it.

Of course, such examples are only the tip of the iceberg. We've all experienced countless people who believe the school can solve all of society's problems, that education is all about keeping score—and a host of other misconceptions, misperceptions, misimpressions, and bald-faced lies.

All of these people are missing important points. They don't get it. But it's not their fault. They don't have reason or resources to grasp the big picture. But who does? Well, you do!

No one else knows what you know or sees what you see. No one else represents all the parties involved or is committed to serving all the constituencies. No one else knows what it's really like. No one else cares as much as you do or has the passion you have. No one else knows what matters most.

At the end of the day, you are the only one who is held accountable. And you are the only one paid to get it right.

That's why you can't just sit still and let others (the amateurs) pick the destination and chart the course for public education.

It's your job to participate in the dialogue, educate the participants, shape the conversation, see that the right questions get asked, and influence the answers.

That's why they call you a school leader, not a school follower. If you abdicate this responsibility, you may get the schools you deserve; but the children won't.

There's a reason that coaches don't like Monday morning quarterbacks. Second-guessers don't fully understand the game; they don't really know the play and the players; and they're suckers for simplistic solutions. The same is true of most vested or special interest groups in education.

For example, if education policymaking is left entirely to politicians, don't expect logic or lucidity. These are not necessary components of the political process. As former New York City Mayor Rudy Giuliani explains, "Those who spend their entire life in politics often become spin artists, rather than thinkers." What's needed in schools today, however, are thinkers, not spin doctors. That's where school leaders should come in.

This is true in any situation where laypeople control the outcomes. Without some professional input and guidance (notice I didn't say professional domination), the result is often a profusion of confusion.

Lacking professional leadership, it's easy for priorities to become blurred, for money to be diverted or misdirected, and for schools to lose their focus. When this happens, adults may complain, but kids are the ones who actually suffer.

In *Crusade in the Classroom,* Douglas B. Reeves describes what he calls the "dance of the lemons"—what happens when only the weakest teachers are left in the poorest schools:

> ... the least capable gather together under the least acceptable conditions to provide the least education to the students who can least afford to be denied the opportunity to learn.

Reeves could have been writing about what can occur when school decisions are left entirely to outside laypeople.

Of course, the worst scenario is when misguided, misinformed, or downright malicious critics go unchallenged by the professionals who know what's really going on.

It's always easy to criticize from the outside. ("Any fool can criticize, condemn, and complain—and most fools do." —Dale Carnegie, self-help expert) Unfortunately, many people accept criticism as valid even when it is unfounded. And troublemakers always listen to troublemakers, which only multiplies the troublemaking.

Worst of all, many critics are intolerant of divergent views. I recently saw a no-parking sign in a restaurant parking lot that read, "Carryout parking only. Others will be crushed and melted." That's how some critics treat those who question or dissent. Who's supposed to stop these people? Well, *you* are! One of the first laws of school leadership is don't be a pushover.

So in a society where everyone wants a piece of the education action and gets it, and where everyone thinks they know best, what are the expectations for a responsible school leader?

The answer isn't complicated; but it often separates real leaders from wannabes and also-rans. If you want to earn a spot in the leader's circle, stand up, speak out, and be counted. Don't let stupid statements go unquestioned. Insist that people look at the facts and remember the school's real mission. Don't sit back and let half-cocked critics or other ill-informed outsiders set the agenda and define what public education is going to be.

In the best-practice schools, leaders are willing to take on "bigots, bullies, and bamboozlers." Is that the way it is in your school?

Effective school leaders always have an opinion, a position, and a platform. Do you? If the people in your community don't know where you stand and what you stand for, you've forfeited a measure of the mantle of leadership.

Don't be afraid to confront misinformation and falsehoods. Don't let bad ideas or bad advice slide by undetected or unchallenged; tell the real story. Be the conscience of the community when it comes to issues affecting education. Remind people of what's right and what's important. Set the record straight; and keep the critics honest.

Do all this even if it causes discomfort or alienates some people. It's better to rock the boat than to go down with the ship not saying a word.

I would go so far as to say that the role of a superintendent isn't just to serve the school board, but to actually *educate* and *discipline* the board when necessary. They don't teach you that in graduate school. Would you go that far? Do you want to be a leader badly enough to stand up to your school board when it is off base or flat-out wrong?

I've known some superintendents who do. I recall a mentor of mine telling his board, "I can't layoff this principal as you directed. He's devoted over twenty years to this district. He deserves better treatment. If you insist on terminating him, you'll have to let me go, too." That's gutsy. And risky. But it's also leadership.

The point of this discussion isn't that you should act as if you always have the right answers. You don't. Like all the rest of us, you've been appointed, not anointed, to your position. You don't have a monopoly on truth or wisdom. But you are the leader. So lead.

Arrogance isn't an effective leadership trait, but neither is timidity. The best school leaders have confidence in their judgment and the courage to stand up for what they believe. That's what's expected of you, too.

I know sermons are cheap, and you want specifics. So here are some practical ways you can help others get it and more fully understand what's real, what really counts, what's happening, what's needed, and what actually works best in public education:

- Make your voice heard throughout the community on important educational topics. Use the power of e-mail to get your message across. Write letters to the editor, to lawmakers, and to other prominent citizens. If you don't write your representatives at least once every legislative session, you're passing up a built-in opportunity to demonstrate leadership. It pays to keep a mailing list of community opinion-makers, movers, and shakers. Karl Menninger, founder of the famed Menninger psychiatric clinic, always had a select mailing list to which he sent a constant stream of articles, reprints, opinion pieces, essays, and personal notes whenever he wanted to influence opinion or shape decision making. If it was good enough for one of the 20th century's leading psychiatrists, it just might work for you, too.

- Attend public hearings on education issues. Encourage colleagues to do the same. Ask the tough questions. And keep asking.

- Use what John L. Badaracco, author of *Leading Quietly,* calls your "political capital"—your *reputation* and your *relationships* to influence, persuade, and convince lay decision makers to accept your point of view.

- Recruit school board candidates who get it. Don't leave the make-up of your board entirely to chance.

- Support (with contributions, endorsements, and word-of-mouth campaigning) legislative candidates who have a solid and realistic grasp of educational issues.

- Tell lots of "kid stories" to remind decision makers of why schools exist and what they are supposed to be about.

- Use the school's public relations resources to promote worthwhile proposals, defend good ideas, discredit bad ideas, and brag about the right things. Not all press releases should be about the school's athletic accomplishments.

- Make yourself available as an unofficial education advisor to key lawmakers and the local media. When they need a "resident expert" on education, you want it to be you, not some spokesperson for the taxpayers' union.

- Get "your people" on committees, commissions, and advisory boards—wherever education is likely to be considered or discussed.

- Use social situations or opportunities to speak out on current topics affecting education. Even the local barbershop can serve as a sounding board. It is often one of the best forums in town.

If these suggestions don't work, try something else. The point is that most people don't get it—so you have to. And you have to help others get it too. It's your job to help everyone see the truth, make wise decisions consistent with basic community values, avoid foolish mistakes, and do the right thing. If you don't, who will?

This doesn't mean that your take on the world will always prevail. There will be times when you will be outvoted, outranked, or outflanked. But that doesn't give you permission to stop trying.

The biggest men and women with the biggest ideas can be shot down by the smallest men and women with the smallest minds. . . . Think big anyway.

Kent M. Keith, author

Of course, it's not always comfortable or convenient to be the lone voice of reason in an environment of conflicting ideas and charged emotions. And it can be terribly lonely. ("A man who wants to lead the orchestra must turn his back on the crowd." —Unknown)

But the bottom line is that you can't call yourself a leader until you are willing to speak out on controversial issues and champion unpopular causes when you believe in them.

It's seductive and nonthreatening to go with the flow, to go along, to get along. I'm sure you can keep your job, keep your title, collect your pay, finish your career, and retire just fine by sitting on the sidelines, letting others make the choices and dutifully carrying out their decisions.

But if you believe even half of what's in this book, that's not good enough. That's not a leader's way.

Real leaders don't settle for waiting to see what happens or just letting things happen. They want to make things happen. After all, education is too important to be left to amateurs. Get it?

22 If You're Not Having Fun, You're Doing It Wrong

Most of the time I don't have much fun. The rest of the time I don't have any fun at all.

Woody Allen, actor-director

When the joy of the job is done, when it's no fun trying any more, quit before you're fired.

Malcolm Forbes, millionaire business guru

Find something you love to do and you'll never have to work a day in your life.

Harvey Mackay, CEO, motivational speaker and writer

School leadership is hard work. Work under pressure. Long hours and late nights. It's often unappreciated work. Expectations are extremely high, and pay is relatively low. Executive perks are modest. No limos. No stock options. But if you do it right, it is the most fun you will ever have . . . more fun than any one human being should hope for in this lifetime.

Are you doing it right? Are you having fun yet?

Unfortunately, many school administrators are not. Some are actually miserable in their jobs. How often have you heard colleagues say, "It's not fun any more?" If you or someone you know feels this way, you need to know this: It's not that there isn't fun to be had. It's not the job. It's the jobholder. If you're not having fun doing what you're doing, you're doing it wrong.

The truth is that there are powerful reasons why being a principal or superintendent should be a job filled with joy—and daily portions of old-fashioned fun. The innovative industrialist Henry Ford was right when he said, "There is joy in work." He wasn't talking about working in schools; but he could have been.

There is inherent happiness in this business. Miracles happen every day. Kids learn, grow, and blossom before your very eyes. Lives are salvaged. Life gets better. Good is done. If that isn't fun, what is?

Better yet, little children are naturally playful. They act silly sometimes. Watching them can make you smile or laugh out loud whether you want to or not.

Likewise, teenagers are always exuberant and excited about everything. They will come over the tops of the desks when they are motivated (and sometimes when they're not).

How can anyone be around young people and not have fun? If you are unhappy being leader of the school, maybe you're not spending enough time around the children.

If the joy of learning by itself isn't enough for you, there is lots of other real pleasure simply in helping others, solving problems, and successfully meeting challenges. ("It's kind of fun to do the impossible." —Walt Disney.)

There is plenty of fun to go around in every school. So why are so many top school officials missing out on it? You and I have both known too many administrators who hate to go to work every day because there is no joy in it anymore. How did they get that way?

As with most human behavior (or misbehavior), there are multiple causes. Some principals and superintendents mistakenly feel it is undignified or unprofessional to have fun. Some are too full of themselves or too self-righteous to let their hair down and enjoy themselves on the job. Some just take themselves too seriously. (The trick is to take the mission seriously, but not yourself.)

Others are too insecure to have fun. Still others become too fearful to have fun. And some eventually become too paranoid (sometimes for good reason) to enjoy what they're doing.

A few can never have a good time at work, simply because they are flat-out incompetent and they know it. They're in over their heads. They may have the credentials (e.g., degree, license), but they don't have the psychological or emotional "right stuff" for the job. They don't have the stomach to play for high stakes and win. As an old Texas saying suggests, they're "all hat and no cattle."

But the most common reason that school administrators lose their sense of joy in the job is that they get too far removed from what matters most. When you forget why you became an educator in the first place, it's difficult to enjoy the journey. Whatever the causes, there is a saving grace: Most causes are reversible. Joy is retrievable.

As CEO of the organization, you can choose a "deadly serious" attitude and miss all the fun. But why would you? It only makes the job more difficult, boring, and even numbing. In the phrase "deadly serious," the operative word is *deadly*.

Education shouldn't be grim, but some administrators make it that way—and spoil it for all the rest of us. Fortunately, it doesn't have to play out in that manner. There are ways to make work fun again. They're worth the effort, because this fun thing has a lot going for it. Having fun on the job isn't just "for fun." It has practical applications as well, including the following:

- In their best-selling business book (mentioned earlier, in chapter 16), *Fish: A Remarkable Way to Boost Morale and Improve Results,* authors Stephen C. Lundid, Harry Paul, and John Christensen brought "fun at work" out of the closet for good.

  Using the example of the irrepressible fish mongers at Seattle's Pike Place Market, who became famous for enjoying their work, being playful on the job, and teasing customers and each other while selling more fish than anyone else, the authors make the powerful point *"Work made fun gets done."*

  Wow! When people enjoy what they're doing, they're more productive. Who would have guessed it? As it turns out, it's true on the wharf, it's true in the classroom, and it's true in the principal's or superintendent's office.

  Actually, teachers have known this all along. Kids do better and learn more when they're having fun. So do adults. If you want to boost results in your school, just make it more fun to be there. It starts at the top.

- Fun is infectious. Once infected, it can spread like a virus throughout the organization. If you're having fun, your staff will too. So will the kids.

  If you enjoy your work, mix work and play, and can make fun of yourself, it gives others permission to do the same.

  Teachers and administrators having fun make those around them feel better and do better, too. Students do better for teachers who make work fun; teachers do better for principals who make work fun; and principals do better for superintendents who make work fun.

Fun is win-win. And it's contagious. Why not start an epidemic in your school?

- Poking fun at hypocrisy, pretentiousness, silly bureaucracy, and other internal foibles keeps an organization honest and more humane. What school couldn't use more of that?

Having fun in a difficult job keeps you sane and healthy. Laughter is the best antidote for stress, frustration, and boredom.

- Enjoying your job makes time go faster. (Time flies when you are having—well, you know the rest.)
- When work is fun, everything else goes better ("When work is a pleasure, life is a joy." —Maxim Gorki, Russian writer).

Obviously, making work pleasurable is a good thing. You work too many hours, and life is too short not to have fun. So what's stopping you? What would it take for you to recapture the joy of everyday school leadership?

One of the USAA Insurance Company's "Pride Principles" is "Have fun. If you're not, find out why and change it." These might be good marching orders for all school leaders as well.

If you are one of the many administrators across the country who have grown increasingly cynical, blasé, and pessimistic and you're just not having as much fun on the job as you used to, or you're not having any fun at all any more, you can either passively sink into the abyss or scramble like crazy to climb out ("You can either scrub the floor or stare at the dirt." —*A Servant's Christmas,* a musical history play). Scrambling is more leader-like.

To help rejuvenate the joy of being a school leader, below are fifty of the best ways I know of to sort out what's most important to start doing the job right all over again and to have more fun every day you go to work:

1. Teach a class. Direct interaction with students always gets the juices flowing again. Even a busy superintendent can find time to teach a single course for a quarter or a semester.

2. Attend a Special Olympics opening ceremony. Better yet, volunteer to help with the event. Every Special Olympics competition is a tribute to hope, courage, and pure joy. If this doesn't get your heart pumping, nothing will.

3. Spend more "face time." Deal directly with people more and hide behind electronic connections (e.g., e-mail, voice mail, fax messages, etc.) less.

4. Go where the joy is (e.g., kindergarten classes, student performances, bar mitzvahs, confirmations, commencements, academic award programs, GED ceremonies, Eagle Scout courts of honor). The funny thing about joy is that it rubs off and can be transmitted by osmosis.

5. Do more of what you like and less of what you hate. If the boss can't delegate, who can?

6. Quit worrying about pleasing everyone. It's not going to happen anyway.

7. Keep learning. We've said it before: "There is joy in learning." If you don't know this, you have been in the wrong profession all along.

8. Work on your attitude. That's where the fun begins.

9. Associate with the fun-lovers on your staff. They will lift you up. Naysayers, pessimists, and prophets of doom will only drag you down, and crepe-hangers will bury you if you let them.

10. Be natural. Be yourself. Your true self got you the job; you don't need a phony persona to keep it. Wearing a mask all the time is tiresome and depressing. Being yourself is the most fun of all.

11. Give up on having all the answers. The release and relief you will feel allows you to have more fun than you ever thought possible.

12. Don't try to do it alone. Build a tight-knit team of advisors (your own personal board of directors). Start with your secretary or administrative assistant. As gatekeeper and access-broker, this person has a lot to do with how enjoyable your job will be. I've known superintendents who even advocate that districts hire an administrative team rather than single administrators one-at-a-time. Minneapolis actually used a consulting firm as its superintendent for a number of years. Think about it.

13. Think big and shoot high. In the movie *Toy Story,* Buzz Lightyear's goal was "Infinity and beyond." Why not? It's more fun striving for the impossible than settling for the mundane. And you just might achieve it.

14. Develop what Warren Bennis and Robert J. Thomas, authors of *Geeks and Geezers,* call *adaptive capacity*—the ability to understand context, seize opportunity, and extract wisdom from experience. If you are confident in your capacity to flex, adjust, adapt, and handle whatever comes, you are never paralyzed by fear or immobilized by

anxiety. Failure can even become a friend. When you achieve a "bring it on" attitude, that's when the fun begins.

15. Use your authority to help those who need it most. Start a program for homeless kids. Reach out to immigrant families. Close the achievement gap for minority students. Whatever needs fixing, fix. Helping others is the most fun you'll ever have.

16. Celebrate triumphs and breakthroughs, even small ones. (Your opponents will take care of celebrating your failures.) Celebrations are fun. That's the point.

17. Give credit to those who deserve it. You may be surprised how good it feels.

18. Do the right thing. It's fun, it feels good, and you will sleep better. How do you start? Northwest Airlines advises its employees to begin simply by doing the right thing for the person standing in front of them. And, then, build on that. That works for me. How about you?

19. Mentor a rising star in the profession. There's nothing much more fun than watching a protégé grow, develop, mature, and deliver, knowing that you played a part in shaping a successful career.

20. Quit procrastinating. Finish stuff. The finish line is where the fun is.

21. Define success your way. It's more fun satisfying yourself than trying to meet someone else's preconceived image of what a successful school leader should be.

22. Take your vacation. That's a no-brainer. If you want to have more fun on the job, take some time away from the job. You will feel better, see clearer and feel more up to the challenge when you return.

23. Create a fun-loving environment in the workplace. Don't just give people permission to have fun on the job; jump-start it. Initiate celebrations, "roasts," and other special events. For example, I once worked with a faculty that made fun a priority. We played volleyball together, held wine-tasting seminars, enjoyed progressive holiday "wassail" parties, and even had our own fund-raisers (e.g., car washes) to pay for a retreat to a nationally known mineral springs resort. The more we played together, the better we worked together. When you blur the distinction between fun and work, you move a step closer to creating an unstoppable team.

24. Say "No" to excessive demands and requests. Focus your energies. You will achieve more, be more relaxed, and feel better about how you spend your time.

25. Attend national professional conventions regularly (e.g., AASA, NAESP, NASSP, and ASCD). These are the granddaddies of educational conferences. Practice selective attendance, network, get inspired, and have fun. It's too good a deal to pass up.

26. Take a tip from the Boy Scouts of America and always be prepared. Preparation is a key to self-confidence and success. When you're thoroughly prepared, even the toughest situations can be fun. Former New Your City Mayor Rudy Giuliani suggests four hours of preparation for every hour of performance. You have to come up with the formula that works for you.

27. Make dreams come true. For example, bend the rules to allow a student from a poverty-level minority community to become the first member of his family ever to graduate from high school; or facilitate the mainstreaming of a severely disabled student whose family desperately wants a regular education for their child. One of the perks of authority is the ability to do good. Use it. There just isn't any greater fun than fulfilling someone's lifelong wish.

28. Don't read all your bad press. How much fun is that? I recall the superintendent of a major city school system saying, "I don't read all the papers any more. If I read one more story about my salary, I'll throw up." She was right. Too much negativity is unhealthy. Great actors don't read all their bad reviews. Instead, they concentrate on improving their performance. School leaders should do the same.

29. Know your limits. Avoid falling victims to the "Peter Principle" (being promoted to your level of incompetence).

    I learned this lesson from a friend who was a superstar teacher and, later, an outstanding junior high school principal. When he was selected as high school principal, everyone (including himself) was confident that he would be a success.

    It didn't turn out that way. What worked in the classroom and as principal of a smaller school for preteens didn't work so well in the more sophisticated and complex culture of a large metropolitan senior high school.

    For a few years, my friend struggled with the job. He wasn't happy. He wasn't having any fun. And he wasn't as effective as he had been in other situations. Finally, he determined it was time to switch jobs.

    He was still a talented educator—just not an A+ high school principal. (Incidentally, he went on to succeed in other assignments and to complete a distinguished career.)

There is no shame in knowing when you're in over your head. Likewise, there is no fun in trying to be what you are not cut out to be.

30. Take time or make time to think. You will enjoy the job more if you can reflect, ponder, plan, and dream about how to do it better. Leadership requires thought, not just shoot-from-the-hip action or knee-jerk reaction.

31. Choose the high ground (". . . always recognize the highest and the best." —St. Paul in a letter to Philippi). Distance yourself from nasty politics, ethical compromises, self-aggrandizement, or exploitation of authority. It's always more fun to be one of the few people in the organization who can sleep peacefully at night.

32. Have lunch with the best people on your payroll. Not just teachers, but custodians, cooks, secretaries, clerks, aides, and bus drivers as well. Their passion and enthusiasm will buoy you up.

33. Keep a journal of meaningful vignettes from your daily experiences. It can help you remember the good times during the bad times. And who knows, you may write a book some day.

34. Live where it's most comfortable for you. Some administrators choose to live in the district where they serve, so that they can participate fully in the community and have a safe haven close by to escape to for occasional relief. Others prefer to live out of their district, so they can get away from their constituents and their family can be spared some of the inevitable rumors and criticism. It's your call.

35. Follow the advice of legendary investment guru Warren Buffet (the Oracle from Omaha)—
    It's O.K. to be wrong.
    Focus on what you know best.
    Worry about information you feel sure of.
    Be patient.
    Keep it simple.

    If it helps business leaders succeed and have fun on the job, it can work for you too.

36. Don't get into disputes with the media. You can't win. As one of my main mentors, Carl Holmstrom, used to say, "Don't argue with someone who buys ink by the barrel."

37. Find out the stories (anecdotes) behind your statistics. Work is more meaningful when you put a face on the data.

38. Don't put up with excessive abusive behavior by parents or the public. School administrators have to put up with a lot of things; but uncivil, insulting, or combative behavior isn't one of them. I've known school leaders to shut down a meeting and clear the room (calling security if necessary) when a public hearing turned nasty or got out of hand. It's gutsy, but it's the right thing to do.

39. Have fun with the budget. Balance it if you can—that's the most fun of all. Otherwise, use it to accomplish lofty goals. Business columnist Ross Levins cites three lessons from the famous writer Henry David Thoreau that can help—
    Spend on things that matter.
    Save for things that matter.
    Give to things that matter.

    These directions could serve as valuable budget guidelines for you and your school board.

40. Search out silly rules, policies, and practices (Stupid Educator Tricks). When you find them (and you will), laugh at them and then fix them. This is fun for everyone.

41. Take some risks. Surprise people—including yourself. That will get the adrenaline flowing every time.

42. Be sure your job is a good fit. No matter how good you are, every job is not a perfect match. Some schools or districts may be too small, or too large. Or too conservative. Or too liberal. Or just don't feel right. You can't have much fun if you are in the wrong job.

43. Innovate. Be the first administrator on the block to have some new program or service. Even in tough budget times, it is still possible to implement some enhancements. If you're fishing for ideas, here are a few possibilities and choices that have proved popular in other leading schools:
    Montessori-type programs
    Cyber-school programs delivered by the Internet
    Project-based leadership training in partnership with Volunteers of America
    Flight simulation training
    International Baccalaureate programs
    Environmental studies

    Innovation energizes everyone involved. It is an elixir for the entire organization.

44. Personally escort visitors to see the best sights and scenes your school has to offer. Bragging and showing off are among life's greatest joys.

45. Visit with successful alumni from your school. Their lives make it all worthwhile.

46. Respect the craft. If you truly appreciate the significance of your profession, you'll realize how much fun it is to be part of it.

47. Network with the best in the business. They won't let you forget the fun of being a school leader. If you want to make the most of mentoring and do something different, try the model that works for the Business Network International in California: Gather up to 40 school leaders weekly during lunch or breakfast. Each person gets one minute to give a "commercial" for his or her school or district. One or two members are chosen each week to give a five-minute talk on some aspect of educational leadership, and the meeting concludes with each participant giving testimonials or referrals. That's real mentoring. And that's fun!

48. Forgive your enemies. Bearing old grudges sours your disposition and robs you of the capacity to enjoy the job.

49. Always have an Exit Card (somewhere to go). Everything is more fun when you have a fallback position.

50. Do a little of what matters most very day. That's the greatest fun of all.

The reason for considering the measures above is that fun on the job is a choice—your choice.

It's OK to share the humor of daily struggles, to be silly at work occasionally, to laugh out loud at the hallowed halls called school, and to find the lighter side of a demanding profession. In fact, it's a prerequisite to surviving and thriving as a principal or superintendent.

Look at the most exciting, successful, and inspiring school leaders you know: They're all having fun. They don't check their playfulness and laughter at the schoolhouse door. Hal Urban (*Life's Greatest Lessons*) is right: "Work and fun are not opposites."

When being a principal or superintendent ceases to be fun, it's not worth it. If that happens to you, it's time to rediscover the joy or quit. Muddling through feeling discouraged, disillusioned, and depressed should not be an option. The writer Rita Mae Brown says it best:

I believe you are your work. Don't trade the stuff of your life—time—for nothing more than dollars.—That's a rotten bargain.

If you're not having fun, you're not only doing something wrong—you're wasting your time and your life. You deserve better. So do your students.

23

Things Are Never as Bad as You Think They Are, and You're Braver, Stronger, and Smarter Than You Imagine

I'm very brave generally, only today I happen to have a headache.

Tweedledum, in Lewis Carroll's
Through the Looking Glass

Life only demands from you the strength you possess. Only one feat is possible—not to run away.

Dag Hammarskjöld,
Former UN Secretary General

Wghat is this title all about? What does it mean? And what is it doing here in a book about survival values and what matters most for school administrators?

It's not a puzzle. There's nothing cryptic about the title. It means what it says. Your worst dreams, as a school leader, are just that—dreams. And if you should ever wake up and find they're real—not to worry—you've got what it takes to handle them anyway.

So why is it important to keep this image on your radar screen? Because doomsday thinking and self-doubt are two of the greatest cripplers that afflict school administrators.

Together, underestimating self and overestimating the potential for calamity are major causes of fear and timidity, which lead to executive paralysis—the inability to make decisions or take action. The results are choices narrowed, opportunities missed, risks not taken, conversations never held, questions unasked, decisions unmade, and problems worsening while waiting for solutions.

I don't believe for a minute that this is the leadership process you have in mind for your school. That's why this topic is included here in a book about what matters most for school leaders.

A timid leader is an oxymoron and a fearful leader has been robbed of hope. You don't want to be either. You don't have to be. No one does. It starts by realizing that problems, setbacks, and crises are rarely as bad as they seem.

How often does the worst-case scenario actually happen? Never. Otherwise, we wouldn't be here to discuss it.

Unfortunately, educators are notorious worrywarts and crepe-hangers. That's why some administrators spend way too much time gnashing their teeth and wringing their hands, when they could be making things better, solving problems, cleaning up messes, and practicing damage control.

The truth is that what we worry about most happens the least. So worry is worthless, and a "disaster mentality" is needlessly immobilizing.

Two experiences early in my career drove home this lesson in ways I'll never forget.

When I was just a novice administrator, I used to lose sleep over worst-case budget projections that indicated future deficits too horrific to handle.

How was the system going to survive when the district would be millions of dollars in the hole within a few years? I wondered why my seasoned colleagues weren't more upset or panicky, until some wise mentor taught me that doomsday budget forecasts never come true.

The mere fact that deficits are projected means that they won't happen, because corrective measures (e.g., belt-tightening, tax increases, greater economies, school-closings, layoffs) will be taken to head off calamity. That knowledge alone can free you up to become a more creative and effective administrator. It worked for me.

The lesson was reinforced years later when, in its infinite wisdom, our state government passed pay equity legislation requiring that public sector jobs of "comparable worth" receive equal compensation.

Female employees (typically cooks, clerks, secretaries) rejoiced. Some male employee groups (custodians, maintenance personnel) scoffed. Since I was responsible for all contract negotiations at the time, I just threw up my hands in despair. How could we objectively quantify the comparable worth of diverse jobs? Who is to say if a playground aide position is worth more or less than a bus driver? How could we convince different unions to agree to a job evaluation process, accept the outcomes, and negotiate wage settlements that provided hefty increases for some and no increases, or even rollbacks, for others?

It couldn't be done. Morale would unravel. Strikes would occur. Mutiny would ensue. I thought the situation was futile. I remember saying more than once, "It won't work. The only solution to comparable worth is death!" And I meant it.

Surprise! I was wrong. It's called being a slow learner. Although it wasn't easy, it all worked out. Ultimately, all positions were ranked and rated according to a decision-band process, and a single salary schedule was implemented for both male-dominated and female-dominated bargaining units.

I finally got it. Have you? The worst case can only happen if you let it, by just worrying instead of working to prevent or correct it. Circumstances can be bad. Really bad. They can be difficult. Very difficult. But they are never—I repeat—never impossible.

When things look like they can't get any worse, they don't. They get better. It's when things are darkest that you are better able to see the emerging light ("The eye is composed of light and dark. But you only see from the dark part." —Rabbi Joseph Potasnick, speaking at a post-September 11 memorial).

The moral is: Worry less and work more. In the Kansas farm country where I grew up, they used to say, "Quit bitchin' and start pitchin'." That's a leadership lesson you don't want to ignore or forget. But that's only half of the lesson. It gets ever better.

Educators do not only waste time and energy worrying about misfortunes that never happen, they also misjudge their own capacity to deal with difficulty. Self-doubt is a common occupational hazard in our profession—as it is in all leadership fields. School leaders experience it most when the stakes are highest (e.g., taking a new job, trying to pass a desperately needed bond issue). You know the feeling.

As it turns out, self-doubt is another wasteful drain on mental and emotional resources. It isn't worthwhile allowing misgivings about your ability to make you hesitant or tentative. The truth is that most of us are "enough" (smart enough, tough enough, and just courageous enough) to handle whatever comes.

In *Leading Quietly,* Joseph L. Budaracco, Jr., describes a continuum (or pyramid) of heroism. At the top are a few superheroic figures. In the middle are a larger number of everyday folks. And at the bottom are even more bystanders, shirkers, and cowards.

In America's public schools, there probably are not a great many larger-than-life heroes. But, fortunately, there aren't a lot of bystanders, shirkers, and cowards either. Most of us fall somewhere in the middle of the heroic scheme of things. And that's plenty good enough.

Principals and superintendents don't have to slay dragons, but they do have to face a variety of demons, great and small. To be a successful school leader, you don't have to be the bravest and strongest warrior on the battlefield or have the highest IQ in the county. But you do have to possess the inner strength and intelligence to make difficult calls, stand up for what's right, and do what has to be done—every day.

Being enough is mostly a matter of maintaining an "I can" attitude. If you think you can, you can. This doesn't mean that you can never be afraid. A little fear is a good thing. It provides the necessary adrenaline for peak performance.

Everyone experiences some fear and has butterflies in their stomach in times of trouble, stress, or pressure. As Giles Theilman, former curriculum director for Topeka, Kansas, once explained, "The trick is to get all the butterflies flying in formation." If you can do that, you'll get by—no matter what.

Heroic leadership doesn't always come in the form of Herculean strength, overpowering brilliance, or courageous acts of mythical proportion, but in small everyday acts that help children and improve schooling. You see and hear about examples on a daily basis.

We've all heard about the teacher in Piper, Kansas, who refused to pass students who plagiarized their final science projects, even though it cost her her job. That's heroic.

More recently, I read about a teacher who stood up to a teenage school shooter who had just killed some of his classmates. The teacher disarmed the student simply by saying, "Stop," and demanding that the shooter's gun be handed over to him. That's heroic.

I've known a superintendent who faced down a black militant leader who threatened, "I can burn down this town in an hour." And another who talked angry union members out of going on strike. That's pretty heroic stuff.

I've also seen a school leader lay off a tenured teacher who was a personal friend, and, at another time, recommend the closing of a popular school—because these things had to be done. That's heroism, too.

But you don't have to look that far from home for examples. Look in the mirror. You perform acts of courage and intelligence every day without even knowing it. (Sometimes, just showing up is the most heroic act of all.) How long has it been since you—

- Stood up to an irate parent
- Intervened for a friend
- Bet on an idea
- Took a calculated risk
- Initiated a significant change over opposition
- Took responsibility for an unpopular decision
- Admitted a costly mistake

If you have done any of these things, you've proved yourself "enough" for the job.

If you're like most school administrators, you didn't start out as heroic; but sometimes circumstances reveal the hero hiding inside ("I am not the lion, but it fell on me to give the lion's roar." —Winston Churchill).

There are reasons why so many school leaders rise to the occasion in challenging situations. Most of the people who enter the education profession have "ethical fidelity" (a commitment to doing the right thing), a strong work ethic (a desire to finish the job no matter what), and a caring attitude. Educators find the courage and smarts they need, not because they are reckless (cavalier) and don't care what happens, but because they care so much.

In addition, if you are still plagued by self-doubts, there are steps you can take to prepare yourself to face adversity and to prop yourself up when trouble strikes. Following is a sample of common survival strategies. Try them. They work:

- Surround yourself with great people—including some who are braver, smarter, and stronger than you. Together, you're equal to any challenge. It's lonely at the top, but you are never truly alone if you have developed an awesome support team.
- Call on the organization's "Institutional Memory"—the experience of previous administrators who got through similar situations. They were mere mortals. And they survived. So will you.
- Remain calm. Control your emotions. Remember, common sense is your greatest ally.
- Radiate confidence. There is power in certainty. It's important to send the message to students, staff, and the community, "I'm confident, so you should be too." If you really aren't all that confident, fake it anyway

("Pretending to be courageous is as good as the real thing." —David Letterman, following September 11, 2001).

- Go public with the problem and publicly announce your plans. Once it's "out there," you have to follow through and deliver on your promises.
- Remain philosophical. It is what it is. You are accountable for your best effort, not for guaranteed specific outcomes. New York City's former mayor Rudy Giuliani advises, "Do what's possible and try what's not." That's all you can do. Then, whatever will be, will be. Life will go on regardless.
- Involve your administrative team in training on trust-building and facing fears. It really does help.
- Try self-affirmations (e.g., "I'm ready." "With my team I can handle whatever comes."). Become your own best cheerleader. It actually can make you feel more confident. On TV's *Saturday Night Live,* Al Franken used to make fun of such affirmations ("I'm good enough; and, by golly, people like me."), but in the real world, they're serious lifelines. I know school leaders who attribute much of their success to self-talk. You probably do too.
- Put things in perspective. Will the world keep spinning? Will this matter much later on?
- Renew effort. The single most effective response to any setback or pending disaster is simply to work harder.

It's OK to use aids like those above or anything else that makes you feel more capable and confident. If a security blanket or a teddy bear will help, use them too.

School leadership is a brutal, bruising, difficult, pressure-filled job. It's much more taxing and stressful than most people begin to realize. That's what makes it so great.

But all this doesn't mean that ordinary people can't do it. They can. Ordinary people do extraordinary things all the time.

The important point is that you don't have to be a super action hero to be an effective school leader. You just have to be enough. And you are. Don't shortchange your capabilities.

If you are brave enough and intelligent enough to realistically size up the enormity of the job and to face your own shortcomings, you're brave enough and intelligent enough to do the job. Don't be intimidated, cowed, awed, or scared off. As one of my favorite elementary directors used to say, "Just press fiercely forward."

In the Disney movie *Pooh's Grand Adventure,* Christopher Robin has some wise words of encouragement for the creatures of the forest. He could just as well have been talking to the creatures in school administration. His words apply to all of us as well.

Here's what Christopher Robin said that all school leaders should never forget: "You're braver than you believe, stronger than you seem, and smarter than you think."

Don't just read the words. Take them to heart. After all, who are we to pooh-pooh Pooh?

24 You Work to Live, Not Live to Work

By working faithfully eight hours a day you eventually get to be a boss and work twelve hours a day.

Robert Frost, America's poet

. . . the purpose of your life is not to serve your business, but the primary purpose of your business is to serve your life.

Michael E. Gerber, baby food business magnate

We lose touch with what counts most—family, fulfilling work, giving of self, achieving dreams and creative goals.

Hyrum R. Smith, author of *What Matters Most: The Power of Living Your Values*

No one gets out of this world alive, so the time to live, learn, care, share, celebrate, and love is now.

Dr. Leo Buscaglia, self-help guru

Being a school leader is a destination position. I know one retired administrator who won't even respond when asked, "Would you do it all over again?" He believes the role of principal or superintendent is too important to even dignify such a question with an answer.

You do the most important work in the community—maybe in the nation. Nevertheless, as it turns out, what's most important isn't work after all. You don't live to work; you work to live. No other job tops yours. But it's still a job.

There's more to life than work. The best school leaders know it. And they want it all. I'm sure you did too at one time. What about now? You know how to lead. Do you know how to live?

Two of the best superintendents I've ever known worked just a few miles apart. One sacrificed family life and all other interests to devote full-time to the job. The other worked hard, but took off weekends and used all his vacations to spend time with family, volunteer in his church, contribute to the community, work for his favorite civic club and local charity, and have fun. Both were successful school leaders. But who was the most successful human being? Who left the greatest legacy?

The job of running a school or a school district is difficult and getting more difficult. It requires an enormous time commitment. Like executives in other fields, principals and superintendents are working longer and harder than ever before. But the administrators you want to emulate most still do a lot more than just work.

The smartest and most successful school leaders discover quickly and early on that the first order of business must be to develop, cultivate, nurture, and care for themselves as professionals, family members, community members, and well-rounded human beings. Living a balanced life is another well-kept secret of sustained, successful school leadership.

You have to manage yourself before you can manage anything else. Good leaders do more than just lead. They live. They balance their inner and outer lives and make room on a regular basis for family, faith, and fun.

Unfortunately, some school officials mistake workaholism for leadership. They're wrong. Working all the time doesn't make anyone a better leader. It just makes them a wrung-out, strung-out, worn-out, and stressed-out leader. It's not the number of hours you put in; it's what you put into your hours at work that really counts.

Workaholism isn't leadership. It's a disease. It even has its own 12-step program.

When you permit your job to define you, you shortchange yourself. If the job becomes all consuming, there is no time left to experience, enjoy, strive for, or dream about anything else. Workaholism is not the path to respected leadership. A better route is a well-rounded life.

Healthy leaders make the best leaders. As it turns out, health is holistic. Good health takes more than a positive work life. It requires physical and mental well-being, wholesome relationships on and off the job, a supportive home environment, and spiritual serenity.

That's why popular author Rick Warren says, "Blessed are the balanced, they will outlast everyone."

Apparently, Robert Fulgham's advice in *All I Really Need to Know I Learned in Kindergarten* was right on target: "Live a balanced life—learn some and think some and draw and paint and sing and dance and play and work every day some." The next time someone tells you, "Get a life," maybe you should pay attention. You can't put off living until you are ready.

Some schools have had success building their staff development program around a "Wellness Wheel," including work environment, physical health, mental health, supportive relationships, community service, play (fun), and spirituality. It's a concept you can use for your own personal development.

Of course, everyone needs work to provide motivation, growth, challenge, accomplishment, recognition, success, advancement, validation, and economic rewards. But work alone doesn't make a healthy—or effective—leader.

It should go without saying that physical health is a cornerstone of success in any field. But many administrators act as if they don't care.

They work too hard. They don't eat right. They don't exercise enough. They don't get enough sleep. And they try to "tough out" periods of extreme stress. They're not being heroic or stoic. They're being foolhardy and short-sighted.

School leadership isn't a death wish. If you don't take time to care for your physical well-being, sooner or later you'll be taking time to recover from serious illness. What kind of role model is that?

You are your own greatest resource. To get the most out of yourself, you need to pay attention to proper diet, adequate exercise and fitness activities, moderate substance use, stress reduction, sexual health, and lifestyle management. (Unless you're in prison, you are the only one in charge of your lifestyle.)

Many principals and superintendents make a mistake when they don't take care of themselves first in order to take care of business later. Don't be one of them.

It gets worse. While too many school leaders ignore their physical health, even more pay little or no attention to their mental well-being.

Good mental health is built on positive self-worth, an optimistic attitude, affirmation and acceptance from others, and unconditional love. The job of school administrator doesn't always provide these ingredients in sufficient quantity. No job can.

That's why truly effective leaders take time away from work to gain perspective and preserve and restore their mental resources.

If you're in it for the long haul, take care of your mental health, just as you do your physical condition. The volatile, emotional, fast-paced, and politically charged world of school leadership today is crazy enough without adding any instability or insanity of you own.

Of course, nothing contributes more to overall physical and mental health than positive and supportive relationships on and off the job. Yet there is nothing that school leaders who work too much shortchange more than their relationships with family, loved ones, friends, associates, and acquaintances.

I know several principals and superintendents who have better relationships, stronger bonds, and closer ties with their assistants at work and the school board than with their own family and closest friends. You know who I am talking about. You may even be one of them. How pathetic is that?

Too often, school leaders make lousy husbands, wives, parents, or close friends. In a recent Parent Self-Quiz conducted by Search Institute and the YMCA of the USA, 50% of parents revealed that they lack a strong relationship with their spouse or partner. It's probably much worse for busy school leaders. But it doesn't have to be that way.

Absence is not a relationship-building or parenting strategy. You owe your family more than your salary. You owe them more of yourself. More importantly, you owe yourself more than hard work, long hours, and late nights at the office.

If you see more of the people at work than you do of your loved ones and dearest friends, your life is out of balance. It's not healthy. It's not necessary. And it's not worth it. Fortunately, you can do something about. It may be easier than you think.

In *The Purpose Driven Life,* Hal Warren reminds us of the "nine characteristics of Biblical Fellowship":

- Authenticity (sharing honest feeling)
- Mutuality (encouraging each other)
- Sympathy
- Mercy
- Honesty
- Humility
- Courtesy
- Confidentiality
- Frequency (building strong relationships takes time, proximity, and repeated personal contact)

Working on improving these characteristics is the way to restore and bolster relationships with people who are important to you at work, at home, in the community, and elsewhere. You will be a better, happier, more rounded person—and a more effective leader—if you do.

One of the best ways to seek out, develop, and enrich relationships is to get involved in community service. Marian Wright Edelman, founder of the Children's Defense Fund, says, "Service is the rent we pay for living." That's why most long-lasting school leaders give back to the community in exchange for all the community gives to the school. If you don't have time to help meet community needs, the community may tire of meeting the school's needs.

There are many other good reasons to help out in the community—

- It's expected. It's what good citizens do.
- It allows you to showcase and use your talents in new and different ways.
- It is an added way to connect with the community and to better understand community problems other than educational issues.
- It provides an opportunity to meet new people and learn additional skills.
- It enhances your reputation, which carries over to the public's image of the school.
- It feels good. It promotes self-satisfaction that you can't get any other way.

But, most important, it's the right thing to do. Look around. It's always the busiest (and most respected) leaders who are first in line to "pay their rent."

In addition to service and the other serious components of a balanced life, there needs to be plenty of room for fun. Otherwise, life becomes drudgery. Who needs it? You know what all work and no play did to Jack. It can do the same to you.

All the great minds, from antiquity ("Play so that you can be serious." — Anacharsis, 600 BC) to modern times ("Play is one of the effective ways to simplify life." —Albert Einstein), have recognized the power and necessity of play. You should too.

If you never have any fun, you are not going to be much fun to work for. That's a liability. All the most successful administrators you've ever met worked hard, played hard, and had fun along the way.

What they know—that some all-business, no frills, stern taskmasters don't—is that this is the only time of their lives, so they might as well have a good time. It won't come around again.

Finally, no life is completely balanced without a strong spiritual component. All grounded, well-rounded leaders make time to develop their spiritual side (e.g., values, morals, ethics, philosophy of life's purpose and meaning, view of eternity, and relationship to a higher power). All great leaders have a spiritual base.

Some administrators mistakenly think that faith and leadership in the public schools don't mix. They're mistaken or misguided or both.

Even in the secular world of business, more and more CEOs and other leaders are embracing spirituality in the workplace and practicing value-centered leadership.

Prayer and study groups and other faith-based activities are springing up in offices throughout the nation's major cities (e.g., Bible study groups at General Mills, designated prayer and meditation rooms at Cargil, and both Jewish and Christian networks among American Express personnel). If spirituality fits with business leadership, it can surely have a place in your life as a school leader.

If you are one of many who have distanced yourself from faith matters, it might be time to reconnect with your spirituality. Try religion or spirituality again. Learn how to pray all over again. Set aside a fixed time for meditation. Seek out quietude, and associate with people connected to causes bigger than themselves.

After all, what you believe and how you live is at least as important as how you manage a budget or administer discipline. Spirituality can make a difference in your life. And it will show in your leadership.

Now, if you are like some readers at this point, you may be thinking, "All this talk about a balanced life is well and good; but I don't have time for a life. I've got too much work to do!"

That's rubbish! It may be a good excuse, but it's not a valid reason. You have all the time anyone else has. How you use it is up to you.

Many principals and superintendents live full, interesting, rich, and well-rounded lives—and are star performers on the job as well. You can do the same thing.

A good time to start would be now. You will always be too busy if you allow yourself to be. Jonathon Lazear, author of *Meditations for Men Who Do Too Much,* laments, "I don't want to spend my days promising myself that there will be time just as soon as I complete . . . whatever." You don't want that either.

You can balance your life. Only you can balance your life. You'll be a better leader if you do.

Other school leaders find, make, steal, create, borrow, or carve out time for work, play, family, friends, community involvement, and a spiritual life. There is no law stopping you from doing it too. The time is here. What may be lacking is the will.

I don't want to write another time-management manual. There are plenty of good ones on the market already. But the following thoughts may get you started.

Time management is only a matter of good choices and good habits. Hal Urban, author of *Life's Greatest Lessons,* explains that winners and losers use time differently—

Losers	Winners
Kill time	Use time
Waste time	Lose time
Squander time	Value time
Can't find time	Organize time
Take time for granted	Treasure time
Let time slip away	Schedule time
Make time	Spend time wisely

If you're interested in a balanced life, you want to be in the "winners" column. It starts by minimizing lost time.

A recent survey, conducted by Priority Management Systems, pinpointed the "Top Ten Time-Wasters" for executives and managers (that includes you):

1. Shifting priorities

2. Telephone (including cell phone) distractions

3. Lack of clear direction or well-defined objectives

4. Trying to do too much

5. Drop-in interruptions (unscheduled visitors)

6. Ineffective delegation

7. Clutter (on you desk or in your mind)

8. Procrastination (lack of self-discipline)

9. Inability to say "No"

10. Meetings

To achieve greater balance in your everyday life, just start working on this list and use the time you save to do what matters most.

Well-known writer Margaret Fuller, perhaps better than anyone else, exposed those leaders who work too much: "Men for the sake of getting a living, forget to live." It's happening to some of your peers and colleagues right now. Don't let it happen to you.

Life is a tough balancing act. But the best school leaders do it all the time. You can too. Here are ten more tips that work for some administrators and just might help you bring more balance into your own life:

- Schedule recreation and family time. Put it on your calendar, "to-do" list, and electronic organizer. Make appointments with family members and friends. And keep them. Respect time allocated to loved ones just as much as you do time set aside for the superintendent or school board members.
- Set boundaries. Actor John Travolta insists on a contract provision that stipulates no shooting on Sundays. Closer to home, one of my mentors told board members up front, when hired as superintendent, that he would not work on Saturdays. And he didn't. Would that work for you?
- Streamline your personal life. Batch similar chores and errands. Divide up daily routines with your spouse, partner, or roommate (e.g., picking up cleaning, getting cash from the ATM machine, grocery shopping). With an equitable division of labor, you will both have more time to do the things you want to do.
- Live in the moment. Pay attention. Take time to appreciate what's going on around you. Don't miss out on your own life ("The trip is about the trip, not the destination." —David Jennings, interim superintendent, Minneapolis).
- Create a Personal Mission Statement to help keep your priorities straight and remind you of what's most important in your life (see example).

---

*Personal Mission Statement (Sample)

My mission is to live my life fully each day, fulfilling all of my obligations, treating others with truth and honesty, seeking to learn more about life and about myself, and striving to make a positive impact on the lives of others.

The following areas will receive special focus and attention at this time in my life:

- Act as a caring, understanding, and loving husband and father.
- Model healthy living.
- Pursue my professional career aspirations.
- Develop old and new friendships.

Self-talk messages:

- Don't be too hard on myself.
- Put my ladders against the right walls.

*Adapted from Jeffrey S. Ramsey's personal mission statement (May, 2003)

- Celebrate "Take Back Your Time Day" and encourage others to do the same. This annual event is a nationwide day intended to challenge Americans to consider how their hurried lifestyle contributes to health problems, family dysfunction, and loss of community. This special day is symbolically scheduled each year nine weeks before year's end to represent the 350 added hours most U.S. citizens put in over what their counterparts in Western Europe work. Appropriately, the event is sponsored by family-value advocates, women's organizations, labor unions, and environmentalists. Of course, one day is not enough. In your mind, you can make every day a "Take Back Your Time Day."

- Work smarter, not longer (e.g., return phone calls between 11:45–4:45. Studies show that this is the time that people are most available, alert, and efficient on the phone).

- Don't take yourself too seriously ("One of the symptoms of approaching nervous breakdowns is the belief that one's work is terribly important." —Bertrand Russell, British philosopher). Actually, your work is terribly important. But you are not. Eventually, you will have successors and the organization will move on without you. So it's OK to take time now for yourself. You deserve it.

- Use your vacation time every time. Vacations aren't luxuries or wasted time. Everyone needs periodical regeneration, rejuvenation, and recreation. (Even the Energizer Bunny needs recharging sometime.)

  They don't hand out trophies for passing up vacation time. No one is keeping score; and no one will long remember your misguided dedication to duty if you forego your vacation ("The ant is knowing and wise; but he doesn't know enough to take a vacation." —Clarence Day, humorist and writer).

  A vacation can replenish the mind, body, and spirit. It provides an opportunity to get reacquainted with your family and gives your staff a break from you.

  The secret is to take your vacation for the right reasons (Hint: It shouldn't be just to please or satisfy others.). Don't take work along, don't call the office every day, and don't make it too easy for your assistants to get hold of you.

  Most principals and superintendents find they actually work better when refreshed by a vacation break. It's too good a deal to miss out on.

- Consider making a "lateral arabesque" (move sideways in the organization). Sometimes if your current position makes unreasonable demands on your time, it helps to make a lateral move to a parallel or comparable position (e.g., principal of a smaller school or an area superintendency) that affords more freedom and flexibility.

What measures (like those above) you may need to take to bring balance back into your life depends on how far out of whack your life was in the first place. Whatever it takes, it's worth it.

This point was recently reinforced for me by the following sermonette passed on by a friend of mine.

A contest was held challenging artists to paint their impression of the true meaning of "Peace." When the winners were announced, second place went to a lovely painting of moonlight reflecting on a placid lake, surrounded by a lush forest, with mountains in the background, and a small doe grazing in a nearby meadow. It was a beautifully serene scene.

But first place went to a picture depicting a raging storm with ominous, boiling clouds, jagged lightening flashes, driving rain, and tree branches wildly thrashing in the wind. It was a disquieting scene, except for a small nest, resting on one of the tree limbs, holding a tiny baby bird inside, fast asleep and oblivious to the tempest surrounding it.

The first picture was beautiful. But it wasn't completely honest or truthful. Real life is more like the second painting.

In the real world, we each have to find or make our own peace in the midst of the many storms that continuously rage around us. At least, that's how it works for most school leaders today.

You won't find that peace at a faculty, PTA, or school board meeting or by working more, longer, or harder. You may find it, however, by having a romantic dinner with your spouse, going to a ball game with your son, laughing with friends, helping out at a charity event, participating in a meaningful church service, or all of the above.

Work is just work. Your job isn't your life—unless you give it permission to be. Don't.

When you look back on your life and reflect on the question "What did you do with your life?" and your only answer is, "I worked," how will you feel?

If you are like most of us, you entered the education profession to be a difference-maker, not just a slave. Sometimes, you have to work less to work better. Living a well-balanced life is the best insurance you can get against irrelevance or insignificance.

The magic of living a balanced life is that by becoming a better spouse, parent, friend, student, citizen, community volunteer, and congregation member, you don't become less of a school leader. In fact, whatever you do to become a more well-rounded person makes you a stronger, more effective leader at the same time.

So what is the message? Simply, that of all the advice in this book, the wisest may be the familiar three little words: "Get a life."

25 It's Worth It!

Leadership is worth the risk because the goals extend beyond material gain or personal advancement.

Heifitz and Linsky, *Leadership on the Line*

It [the superintendency] is a job worth doing.

David Jennings, upon being
named Minneapolis superintendent

School leadership isn't for sissies. It's a grueling job full of trials, tribulations, and trouble, played out in a political quagmire and, largely, underappreciated by almost everyone except kith and kin.

But all these difficulties pale in significance compared to the enormous possibilities for lasting achievement. Everyone wants to make a difference. Principals and superintendents actually do. It's their values that do it.

All of the preceding pages are packed with the principles, priorities, stubborn truths, and life lessons that matter most for school leaders. And now at last, there is one final value that sustains all the rest. What is it? The simple, no-nonsense, non-negotiable notion that—It's worth it!

It is this belief that prompts lasting leaders to slosh on through the muck of petty politics and bureaucracy.

Faith healers have always proclaimed that each of us has within us what it takes to heal ourselves. Likewise, effective administrators have within themselves what it takes to heal the ills confronting public education today. What all good school leaders have internalized are the bedrock beliefs and lasting insights you've been reading about. These are what make the work worthwhile.

Some people want a job. Others want a career. A few want more. They want work that has deep purpose and meaning and the potential for effecting immeasurable good. If you are in this latter category and you are a principal or superintendent, you're where you're supposed to be.

Success as a school official starts with an attitude—an attitude of gratitude. Top administrators are always grateful for the opportunity to leave a lasting legacy. Are you?

If you have any doubts or misgivings concerning the worth of what you do, sometime, when you're working late and the building is quiet, listen to the voices of the ghosts of leaders past. They will all tell you, "It's worth it!"

Thank God, you're a school leader.

A Final Word

The Ouija Board Effect

. . . it is easy for principals to lose touch with the fundamental reasons for why they are in the role.

Michael Fullan, educator-author

Don't settle for just achieving the "good life," because the good life is not good enough.

Rick Warren, author of *The Purpose Driven Life*

Remember the Ouija Board and the games people played with it? Some still do. The Ouija Board has the alphabet and other symbols on it. And it is accompanied by a small, triangular planchette supported by two casters that often hold a vertical pencil.

The premise is that, when lightly touched by the fingers, the planchette mysteriously moves around the board in such a way as to spell out spiritual or telepathic messages or answers.

Obviously, some force (subconscious or supernatural) guides the Ouija Board to the right (desired) response or answer. Believers hold that the messages are revealed by unknown forces, not by the subtle nudging of wishful thinking. Who knows? Who cares? It's just a board game.

School leadership, on the other hand, is the real world with real kids and real problems to be solved. You can't rely on a Ouija Board or Magic 8-Ball for answers. So as a principal or superintendent, what guides, directs, or influences your choices and decisions? Ego? Politics? Ambition? Self-preservation? Job security? Popularity? Fitting in? Or core values that keep you focused for the long haul? (Values give leadership the legs to go the distance.)

Success in any human behavior requires a strong start *and a* strong finish. One of President George H. Bush's mantras was, "Finish strong." That's good advice for a president. It's just as good advice for a school leader.

Most school leaders start off strong—grounded in time-honored values and driven by lofty goals. But, over time, many—more than you and I can count—begin to slow down, ease off, stop taking risks, avoid rocking the boat, and settle for pat solutions and easy answers. To paraphrase T. S. Eliot's words, they end in a whimper, not a bang.

What will it be for your career? Forget the Ouija Board. You have to find answers in yourself. You can either accept "good enough" (mediocrity), wind down, and ease into a comfortable retirement; or you can remain true to your values, even when it is uncomfortable, unpleasant, and unpopular, and finish stronger than ever.

Do you want to finish safe or finish strong? What matters most to you?

Resource A

What Others Say About
What Matters Most

(In School and in Life)

No one has a monopoly on what matters most. Following are what some other important and thoughtful people have to say on the subject.

> *It's easy to get distracted and forget what is most important.*

> Rick Warren, *The Purpose Driven Life*

> *The purpose of life is not to be happy. The purpose of life is to matter, to be productive, to have it make a difference that you lived at all.*

> Author unknown

> *The whole purpose of education is to turn mirrors into windows.*

> Sydney J. Harris, columnist

> *Moral purpose of the highest order is having a system where all students learn, the gap between high and low performance becomes greatly reduced, and what people learn enables them to be successful citizens and workers in a morally based knowledge society.*

> Michael Fullan, Dean of the Ontario
> Institute of Studies in Education

If you want to be successful, it's just this simple: Know what you're doing. Love what you're doing. And believe in what you're doing.

O. A. Battista, author

I think the purpose of life is to be useful, to be responsible, to be honorable, to be compassionate. It is, above all, to matter, to count, to stand for something, to have made a difference that you lived at all.

Leo Rosten, immigrant writer

Many things matter in today's highly competitive marketplace, but a full parking lot at seven o'clock in the morning is not one of them.

Warren G. Bennis and
Robert Thomas, *Geeks and Geezers*

You are not here merely to make a living. You are here in order to enable the world to live more simply, with greater vision, with a finer spirit of hope and achievement. You are here to enrich the world and you impoverish yourself if you forget the errand.

Woodrow Wilson, Former U.S. President

Do all the good you can, by all the means you can, in all the ways you can, in all the places you can, at all the times you can, to all the people you can, as long as you ever can.

John Wesley, founder of Methodism

We're lousy trying to figure out how to export democracy around the world. I'll tell you how: Give them a good public school system. Give every kid an opportunity to work their way up into the middle class and maybe beyond, and democracy will take care of itself. When we're talking about why there's still democracy in this country after 200-plus years, it's in no small part because we've had a public school system.

David Jennings, Interim Superintendent, Minneapolis

I seriously doubt whether one can become a fully formed moral human being without ever taking a stand on a controversial or unpopular issue.

Jeremy Iggers, "Everyday Ethics" columnist

It helps, I think, to consider ourselves on a very long journey: The main thing is to keep the faith, to endure, to help each other when we stumble or tire, to weep and to press on.

Mary Caroline Richard, writer

In spite of illness, in spite even of the arch-enemy sorrow, one can remain alive long past the usual date of disintegration if one is unafraid of change, insatiable in intellectual curiosity, interested in big things, and happy in small ways.

Edith Wharton, American writer and satirist

I always say, 'Keep the main thing the main thing,' and the main thing is about children and their education. Don't get distracted by other interests that aren't important to that.

Carol Johnson, on leaving
the Minneapolis superintendency
to accept a similar position in Memphis.

To be good and do good is the whole duty of man comprised in a few words.

Abigail Adams, wife of President John Adams

Our business as rational human beings is to strive for what ought to be, rather than what is going to be, in the consciousness that it will never be all we want it to be.

Herbert Mueller, *Uses of the Past*

Life is like a stone, skipping over clear water. You don't know how many skips you're going to get, or for how long. What's important are the ripples you make and how they affect the ones around you.

Donna Christenson, survivor of
infection by a flesh-eating illness

Definition of a Successful Life: To laugh often and much; To win the respect of intelligent people and the affection of children; To earn the appreciation of honest critics and endure the betrayal of false friends; To appreciate beauty, to find the best in others; To leave the world a bit better, whether by a healthy child, a garden path or a redeemed social condition; To know even one life has breathed easier because you have lived.

Bessie Anderson Stanley

Resource B

Other Books About
What Matters Most

If you want more or different views of what is most important, you can't go wrong reading the following works. Each is unique and has changed me in some way. They may do the same for you.

Andrews, A. (2003). *The traveler's gift: Seven decisions that determine personal success.* Nashville: Thomas Nelson.

Armey, D. (2003). *Armey's axioms: 40 hard-earned truths from politics, faith and life.* Hoboken, NJ: Wiley and Sons.

Bennett, W. J. (1993). *The adult's book of virtues.* New York: Simon & Schuster.

benShea, N. (2003). *Inspire, enlighten and motivate.* Thousand Oaks, CA: Corwin.

Bronson, P. (2002). *What should I do with my life: The true story of people who answered the ultimate question.* New York: Random House.

Carlson, R. (1995). *What about the big stuff? Finding strength and moving forward when the stakes are high.* New York: Hyperion.

Clark, R. (2003). *The essential "55": Rules for discovering the successful student in every child.* New York: Hyperion.

Covey, S. R., Merrill, R. A., & Merrill, R. R. (1994). *First things first.* New York: Simon & Schuster.

Edelman, M. W. (1992). *The measure of our success.* Boston: Beacon Press.

Elgin, S. H. (1998). *The grandmother principles.* New York: Abbeville Press.

Fulghum, R. (1989). *All I really need to know I learned in kindergarten.* New York: Villard Books.

Fullan, M. (2003). *The moral imperative of school leadership.* Thousand Oaks, CA: Corwin and Ontario Principals' Council.

Fullan, M., & Hargreaves, A. (2003). *What's worth fighting for in your school.* New York: Teachers' College, Columbia.

George, B. (2003). *Authentic leadership: Rediscovering the secrets to creating lasting value.* San Francisco: Jossey-Bass.

Giuliani, R. (2002). *Leadership.* New York: Hyperion.

Johnson, M. (2002). *In the deep heart's core.* New York: Grove Press

Keith, K. M. (2003). *Anyway: The paradoxical commandments.* New York: G. P. Putnam's Sons.

Kushner, H. S. (2002). *Living a life that matters.* New York: Anchor Books.

Levoy, G. (1997). *Callings: Finding and following an authentic life.* New York: Three Rivers Press.

Maxwell, J. C. (1998). *The 21 irrefutable laws of leadership: Follow these and people will follow you.* Nashville: Thomas Nelson.

Nerborn, K. (1996). *Simple truths: Clear and gentle guidance on the big issues in life.* New York: MJF Books.

Roger, J., & McWilliams, P. (1991). *Life 101.* Los Angeles, CA: Prelude Press.

Smith, H. (2000). *What matters most: The power of living your values.* New York: Simon & Schuster.

Urban, H. (2000). *Life's greatest lessons: 20 things that matter.* New York: Simon & Schuster.

Warren, R. (2002). *The purpose driven life.* Grand Rapids, MI: Zondervan.

Resource C

Other Lasting Truths That Couldn't Be Squeezed Into This Little Book

In the complex world of school leadership, there are many lessons to be learned. The house of wisdom is made up of many building blocks. Some of the most basic beliefs, values, and lasting truths for school leaders are covered in the preceding sections. But there are more—many more.

Below are several additional key principles and precepts (unadorned and without amplification) that just didn't quite make the cut for inclusion in the main body of the text. They are still important. You'll see why.

After assimilating these, you may want to start your own list. After all, good leaders never stop learning. (By the way, that's another lasting truth.)

More Lessons

- It's not about you.
- Leadership and popularity are not synonymous.
- You can't please everyone. You don't have to.
- All school leaders have enemies. And that's not a bad thing.
- It's never just about the numbers.
- Relationships are more important than rules and roles.
- Words have power.
- Preparation is a forgotten secret weapon.
- You can't reverse gravity.
- Hard work still pays off.
- Life is neutral.
- Example is the best way to lead.
- You never stop being a teacher.
- Leadership is what you do today.

- The future is negotiable.
- Even bosses have bosses.
- Attraction is better than promotion.
- All schools and their leaders have warts.
- We *know* better than we *do*.

Your List

- _____
- _____
- _____
- _____
- _____

Index

**CORWIN
PRESS**

The Corwin Press logo—a raven striding across an open book—represents the union of courage and learning. Corwin Press is committed to improving education for all learners by publishing books and other professional development resources for those serving the field of K-12 education. By providing practical, hands-on materials, Corwin Press continues to carry out the promise of its motto: "**Helping Educators Do Their Work Better**."